DATE DUE

THE COMPUTER IN GRAPHIC DESIGN

THE COMPUTER IN GRAPHIC DESIGN

FROM TECHNOLOGY TO STYLE

RONALD LABUZ

VNR VAN NOSTRAND REINHOLD
New York

Library of Congress Catalog Card Number 92-9981
ISBN 0-442-00971-2

 I⟨T⟩P Van Nostrand Reinhold is a division of International Thomson
Publishing. ITP logo is a trademark under license.

Printed in Hong Kong.

Van Nostrand Reinhold
115 Fifth Avenue
New York, NY 10003

International Thomson Publishing
Berkshire House
168–173 High Holborn
London WCIV 7AA, England

Thomas Nelson Australia
102 Dodds Street
South Melbourne 3205
Victoria, Australia

Nelson Canada
1120 Birchmount Road
Scarborough, Ontario
MIK 5G4, Canada

16 15 14 13 12 11 10 9 8 7 6 5 4 3 2 1

Library of Congress Cataloging-in-Publication Data

Labuz, Ronald, 1953-
    The computer in graphic design : from technology to style /
by Ronald Labuz.
        p.   cm.
    Includes index.
    ISBN 0-442-00971-2
    1. Graphic arts—Data processing. 2. Computer-assisted
design.
  I. Title.
  NC997.L29   1992   92-9981
  745.4'0285—dc20   CIP

CONTENTS

CONTENTS

There is only one way left to escape the alienation of present-day society: *to retreat ahead of it:* every old language is immediately compromised, and every language becomes old once it is repeated.

Roland Barthes, *The Pleasure of the Text*

PREFACE

For many, the computer is rapidly becoming the preferred medium to produce graphic design. For many others, it is the only way. There is every indication this trend will continue. In the next several years, the computer will overtake traditional methods. Various stages in the ideation, production, and prepress processes will individually give way to the computer. For the second time in history, the basic way we produce visual communication will have fundamentally changed. That is the future history forecast by several of these graphic designers.

The individuals included in this book represent the vanguard of those who have led the way toward a mature use of a new technology. From a beginning of visually awkward work assembled by computer engineers, mathematicians, and scientists, graphic design using the computer has emerged as a composite of several very different aesthetics. This book documents and discusses the work and working practices of those who, in the first fifteen years of the medium, have created significant patterns others will follow. Graphic designers and design firms from Great Britain, Japan, the Netherlands, Czechoslovakia, Germany, and the United States have participated in forging new and different directions. The profession of graphic design has been well served by a multiplicity of individuals who have energetically and enthusiastically created new ways to do old things.

The new technology and the newer style share the history of visual communication with graphic design as a handicraft. In the last decade, it has contributed a new chapter to that history. There is still debate as to whether the computer is just a new tool or does in fact mandate a radically different approach to the designed page. That argument has engendered four different ways to do graphic design with the computer. The technology can be visible in either a primitive or sophisticated manner. We know immediately that a given work was created with a computer. Max Kisman, John Hersey, Rudy VanderLans, and Zuzana Licko are thereby related to April Greiman and Kazumasa Nagai. Other graphic designers favor a less obvious approach. One form of the invisible computer offers the advantages of production speed and control but does not necessitate aesthetic change. The computer graphics of Nancy Skolos, Kenneth Hiebert, or Lance Hidy are not immediately discernible from their work done under a different technological regime. Style carefully forged with thoughtful-

ness and grace is not sacrificed to the new machine. A fourth group requires the computer but, for individualized reasons, do not allow it to visually emerge.

The arrangement of creative individuals within an imposed order is, at times, problematic. Several of these graphic designers have graduated from one of the prescribed visible and invisible forms to another. Several continue to do so as the aesthetic need fits. That freedom does not mean the schemata is an artificial construct. The differences and similarities discussed in this book are real. Moreover, the advantages provided by the construct outweigh the potential problems. This is, first, a reasonable and convenient means to discuss this work in an orderly way. Second, comparisons and contrasts provide a means whereby others can be intelligently influenced. Third, and most importantly, this critical format frames an ongoing debate. What will be the eventual impact of the computer? Will it forever change the way graphic design is done and, as some have argued, the way we think not only about graphic design but about all things? Or is the computer simply a gadget that will make production simpler and faster?

Through their careers as visual communicators, the graphic designers presented in this book have considered these questions. Many answers are given. Some have been wise; some have been more transparent than others. Accepting this work as our collaborative beginning, each of us should develop our own response to these questions of the age. Fortunately, the collaboration between the graphic designer and the computer has quickly produced remarkable results. Judging from this work (and its meaning), the potential of graphic design is as promising and exciting as its past. Everyone interested in our mutual future should be pleased that such a firm foundation has been constructed.

ACKNOWLEDGMENTS

The most important contributors to any book documenting a current of graphic design are the designers themselves. I thank the visual communicators, those who provide the vision and the images. Though many now believe there is no limit to participation, designers remain the ultimate source of these messages. I wish especially to thank those American designers who have struggled to be suggestive. In this country, the good they do is not fully recognized.

I would like to recognize the efforts of those who provided assistance in the development and evolution of this book and others. Lilly Kaufman of Van Nostrand Reinhold has been a consistent supporter. More recently, Amanda Miller has also understood that the literature of graphic design must develop beyond flattering reportage and technical explanations. I thank each of them

for participating in this struggle—an effort that, from different directions, R. Roger Remington and Steven Heller have kept on carrying on. Three recent authors are thanked for their own contributions, both to the design discourse and to computer graphic design. April Greiman, Kenneth Hiebert, and Sumner Stone have each produced wonderful books that every computer designer, amateur and professional, should read and understand.

Don Dempsey and James O'Looney have provided steady guidance in understanding and mastering technology. I thank Steven Rogers for his assistance in preparing photographic art. Leif Allmendinger, Kenneth Hiebert, Johnee Bee, April Greiman and her staff, Takenobu Igarashi, Kazumasa Nagai, and Clement Mok have been particularly helpful in providing graphics. Mark Stress is to be thanked for his assistance in preparing the design of the book. The assistance and support of Mohawk Valley Community College and Syracuse University are gratefully acknowledged.

Finally, it would be presumptuous to fail to mention the counsel of my wife, Carol Altimonte. Her encouragement, advice, patience, and visual good sense were a necessary and essential contribution. In many substantial ways (excepting, of course, the inevitable shortcomings) this project is as much hers as it is mine.

1

THE EVOLUTION OF STYLE

Living in a present consumed by rapid change, it is often difficult to recognize the social and historic value of the recently new. It is easy to forget that the desktop publishing revolution was launched in 1985. Unlike the introduction of lithography in the late eighteenth century or colored markers in the 1960s, or the introduction of any media other than the printing press to mid-fifteenth century Europe, the computer has changed the way images are created *and* the way we think about those images.

We have experienced, and continue to experience, a profound cultural change. The printing press was a seminal invention that helped to foster a new historical epoch, modernism. The computer may prove to be the device that aids in the creation of the epoch that follows. Some argue that modernism is not yet dead. Perhaps this is an argument at cross-purposes, a matter of careful semantic distinctions. But the ways in which we learn, work, create, communicate, and think have undeniably been altered. By the computer

Design is both a process and a product, a noun and a verb. Technology has impacted both senses of the word. Graphic design is challenged by mandated changes in our workways. The most visible result has been the product of this alteration in process: dramatically different imagery. At times, these images are unintelligible to many, if not most. This is a simple problem. Computer imagery is often more difficult to interpret because it is framed in a new form of visual speech. Novelty is dangerous. The sign may be lost in the signifier.

We all must learn the new languages being created for and by new designers. The world has been changed. As Murray Laver has remarked, the traditional three Rs are being replaced by the three Ps: push-button, picture, and program. Computer graphic design has been criticized as idiosyncratic, egocentric, superficial, typographically illiterate, and culturally elitist. The criticisms have often been well-deserved. However, as Meredith Davis has cogently remarked, "competence on the Macintosh is now an entry level requirement to employment in graphic design" (Davis 1991, 20). Computer graphic design is definitely here to stay.

The best computer graphic design is a cultural signpost, informing us about the values and changing structures of our society. Because of the importance of that role, the communicative barriers created by both computerspeak and computerlook are forgivable. Although computer graphic design has

not yet achieved adolescence, the masters of the medium have forged meaningful, insightful, and even poignant messages. More importantly, these messages, at times, could not be created in any other media. Computer graphic design, though culturally problematic, is also necessary.

Gary Ludwig, of The Spencer Francey Group, has framed the aesthetic problem of computer graphic design quite succinctly. "As designers are instilled with the power to do anything, it would be nice if they had the intelligence and taste to do the right thing" (Ludwig 1990, 54). Not all computer graphic designers have the intelligence of April Greiman or Takenobu Igarashi, or the taste of Clement Mok or Nancy Skolos. What is the state of computer graphic design at the moment? Are the appalling graphic afflictions of hordes of amateur desktop publishers worth the price of apparently lonely but master computer designers? On an aesthetic basis alone, is the computer an evil? Should we be latter-day Luddites, fighting against the encroachment of new technology on our workspace? If so, can such a battle realistically be won? These sorts of questions may be quixotic. They are nevertheless real. They reflect the intelligent concerns of many who respect and often cherish the value and need for competent, socially responsible communication.

The computer is neutral. Like the T-square and the triangle, this machine is a tool that may be used poorly or well, responsibly or irresponsibly. Fortunately, the short history of the medium has already produced work of exceptional quality. Rapidly moving from infancy to adolescence, computer graphic design has matured as a medium in a remarkably short time.

The work of the best contemporary computer designers should be admired and emulated. As in any endeavor requiring a combination of skill and decision making, we learn from the work of masters. The pioneering efforts of those who completed the first experiments in computer graphic design cannot, unfortunately, be placed within this category. Early work was marred by poor reproduction quality, insufficient storage capacity, and a reliance on machine capability rather than style or sensitivity. We can and should, however, take some care to understand the efforts of those who worked in the medium's first decade. That work framed some of the questions and problems faced by the professionals who follow.

EARLY QUESTIONS

As early as 1975, the nascent microcomputer offered a glimpse at a future of personal computers and universal usage. But until 1985 and the marriage of desktop publishing and the Apple Macintosh, there was little need for most graphic designers to be concerned with new technology. The computer's impact during the decade between 1975 and 1985 centered on the areas of typesetting technology and newspaper production rather than graphic design. New buzzwords included interfacing, hardwiring, media conversion, the electronic office, and word processing. Most graphic designers, if not completely unaware, were unconcerned about these technological developments.

The first attempts at computer graphic design were marked by an unfortunate combination of limited computer power and undeniably inadequate aesthetics. Many experiments were conducted by engineers and technicians rather than by trained graphic designers. After the first seminar in computer graphic design, sponsored by the Media Laboratory of the Massachusetts Institute of Technology in 1979, more interest was shown. In most cases, that interest did not translate into involvement because of limited access to technology powerful enough to produce valuable results.

The status of computer graphic design in the 1970s, then, was typical of the research and development phase of any new technology. As might be expected, efforts foreshadowed many abilities now current in graphic design. These include the work of the Media Laboratory, Samuel Antupit's 1971 experiments with animation using the Dolphin System, Donald Knuth's METAFONT, work in animation at the Walt Disney Studios and the New York Institute of Technology, and Dynabook. The latter prototype, produced by The Learning Research Group at the Xerox Palo Alto Research Center, was an early experiment in the principles of nonsequential understanding now being popularized through hypermedia.

Pagination technology not dissimilar to today's desktop publishing environment was widely available as early as 1981. The Bedford and Penta front ends were, however, priced far beyond the pocketbook of most users. Systems costing $250,000 or more were interesting marvels to be seen and displayed at equipment shows. Few graphic designers actually used the technology. Large type houses, newspapers, and major magazines were the market for this first generation of wysiwyg (what-you-see-is-what-you-get) display devices. The first computer product to be marketed as a graphic design tool would not be available for another five years. In 1985, the Macintosh breakthrough was not so much technological as it was economic. Affordability rapidly created a new and remarkably expanded level of interest. The designer's experience with the computer was now not limited to demonstrations and exhibits of work done by engineers. Suddenly, graphic designers could actually use the machine to create their own images.

FROM PIXELATED FORM TO INVISIBILITY

The machines of the first generation, before the Macintosh, were largely unavailable. The work done on these machines, however, had some impact. If for no other reason but that both stylistic patterns and specific work

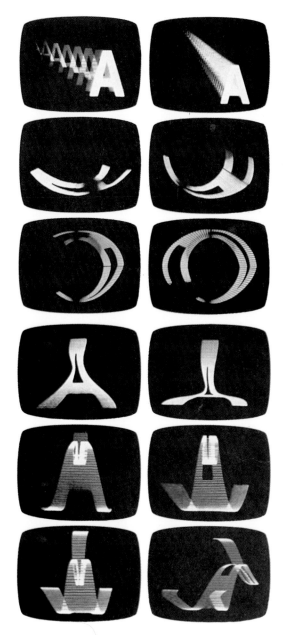

1-1.

Samuel Antupit created variations on the letter "A" using the Dolphin Computer Production and Design System, developed specifically for the production of graphic art and animation. Illustration adapted from Edward Gottschall, *Graphic Communication '80s, 1980.*

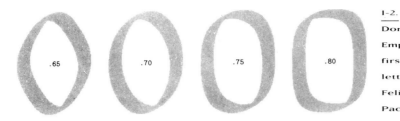

1-2.
Donald Knuth, METAFONT.
Employing a technique
first used by Renaissance
letterers such as Felice
Feliciano, Fra Luca
Paccioli, Damiano da
Moile, Geofroy Tory,
and Albrecht Durer,
METAFONT permits the
user to create and
manipulate alphabets
through mathematical
formulae. The angle of the
superellipse, for example,
creates different shapes
that are repeated in each
letter of a proposed
alphabet. 1986.

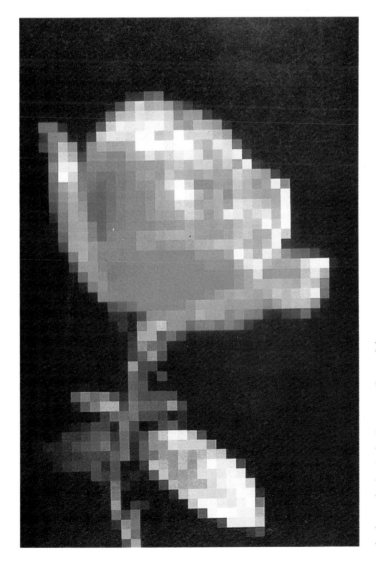

1-3.
Computer graphics circa
1981. Joan Dugan. Calendar
page for the Herlin Press.
Incongruously typeset in
Helvetica, this heavily
pixelated illustration of
a rose was sufficiently
unusual to receive an
award for typographic
excellence. Reproduced in
Typography 3, the Annual
of the Type Directors Club
of New York.

methods had been established, the earliest computer graphic design is of some interest.

The works were most often created by those untrained in graphic design. Moreover, even when professional graphic designers created images, the output quality available to early experimenters was often quite poor. Even if the screen image was aesthetically valuable, the printed image did not necessarily reflect the original intent of the designer or the result as viewed on screen. Working in unfamiliar territory, in retrospect the earliest work resembles the naive work of folk artists: primitive, unschooled, and often amateurish. Although the marks given to this work are not often high, at times individual experiments do feature (as does folk art) the same energy, intensity, and honesty as seen in professional work of lasting value.

The first popular discussion of a computerized design future was published in 1980. *Graphic Communication '80s,* written by Edward Gottschall, the editor of *U&lc* (*Upper and lower case*), first appeared as Volume 7, No. 2 of that controlled circulation magazine, a quarterly published by International Typeface Corporation. With a readership in the tens of thousands, *U&lc* was an ideal vehicle to spread the computer word. The report was later published in book form by Prentice-Hall. Although primarily concerned with text input, storage, and retrieval, this research does offer a glimpse toward the computerized creation of images. Imaging technologies in 1980 centered on the personal (games and hobbies), technical (aviation and drafting simulations), and slide presenta-

1-4.

Computer graphics circa 1983. Andrea D'Amico. The video-palette illustration was prepared and produced by Digital Effects, Inc. (DEI). A pioneer in the creation of computer-generated imagery, DEI was one of four graphics firms (including Information International, Robert Abel & Associates, and MAGI) to participate in the making of the Walt Disney Productions film, *Tron.* Illustration adapted from Joseph Deken, *Computer Images: State of the Art.* New York: Stewart, Tabori & Chang, 1983.

tion markets. At the time, the major areas showing interest in new imaging technology were those concerned with military and space applications, such as at National Aeronautics and Space Administration (NASA), Martin-Marietta, McDonnell-Douglas, and manufacturers of slide presentation equipment, including the Genigraphics system (General Electric) and the Xerox 350 Color Slide System. None of these systems were designed to produce vernacular graphic design.

Emulating Janus, most graphic designers were looking longingly to the past and the future at the same time. Seymour Chwast correctly noted at a 1978 Graphic Arts in Industry trade show that, although the new machines appeared to offer new possibilities, they did not make the task of the graphic designer any simpler: "Laser beams cannot help designers to think, to draw, to find the best way to communicate ideas to other human beings" (Gottschall 1980, 30). Chwast warned his colleagues that the new machine was only a machine, not a saviour. It was capable of producing exceedingly poor and (perhaps worse) uneducated graphics, and

was certainly no replacement for human inventiveness and creativity. This view was by no means a radical one; indeed, even now, some graphic designers continue to completely eschew technology in favor of the pencil or marker.

The opinion that technology necessarily dehumanizes the design workspace was not unpopular in the early and mid-1980s. The battle between those who would and would not use technology, however, was at best a holding action. Attempting to look forward ten years, Gottschall successfully suggested a design future that is now a present: "The main point here is that we are rapidly approaching a time when very versatile, very capable devices will be affordable to all. A generation is growing up with these "toys", much as we grew up with alphabet blocks. . . . When that generation of potential artists comes of age (along with the maturing of these highly capable devices), instead of debating whether computers really are artist's tools, they will wonder how previous generations ever got along without them" (Gottschall 1980, 229).

Before that new (and present) generation could grapple with problems, many strategies had been resolved. Much of the pioneering work required to both develop and humanize computer graphic design was done, and continues to be done, at the Visible Language Workshop of the Media Laboratory at Massachusetts Institute of Technology (MIT).

As an investigating and inventing body, the Visible Language Workshop has taken responsibility for the intelligent exploration of the computer as design tool. The history of the workshop is a microscopic view of the history of computer usage in graphic design. Recognizing that this new medium was nontraditional, Muriel Cooper, the director of the Workshop, has emphasized the interactive and nonlinear aspects of the computer. Many of the opportunities now afforded to the computer graphic designer were developed at the Workshop or by its graduates.

Whether a Bauhaus or a Salon des Refusés for the computer age, the Workshop is "the experimental bridge between the computer and four hundred years of printing" (Heller 1989, 99). The Workshop is a constituent part of the larger Media Laboratory, headed by director Nicholas Negroponte. Although its configuration has changed several times, the Media Laboratory consisted of several research groups in 1990: Human Interface; Epistemology and Learning; Computers and Entertainment; Electronic Music; Performance and Technology; Computer Animation and Graphics; Electronic Publishing;

The Visible Language Workshop; Film/Video; Spatial Imaging; Vision Sciences; Speech Recognition; Advanced Television; and Telecommunications. Because of its experimental diversity, and its experimenters, both available as resources, the Workshop has achieved its basic purpose: to broaden the scope of computer graphic design from a physical to a digital model.

Each new medium emulates the medium it replaces. The typefaces created by Gutenberg in the 1450s were based on the Fraktur calligraphic script then used in Mainz. The first computer software systems produced images that looked like poor copies of traditional messages. The example of the first computer paint systems is instructive: "Early digital paint systems were modeled on physical, analog brushes; the language and behavior of physical and oil watercolor painting were laid on the top of a digital world like a varnish" (Cooper 1989, 9).

The Workshop has stripped the varnish of traditional methods. The truly new and interdisciplinary technologies and processes that have resulted are the identifying marks of computer graphic design. Some of these signatures have not yet been widely accepted by the design public. The pioneering work of Cooper, Ron MacNeil, Walter Bender, David Small, and others at the Workshop have, however, already changed the way we do the things we do.

The operating principle of the Workshop is that "the computer is a totally differ-

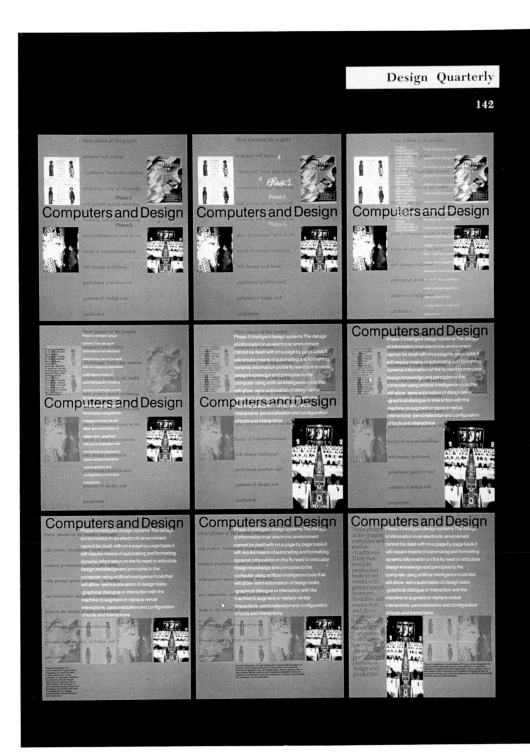

1-5.

Visible Language
Workshop. Cover of
Design Quarterly, Number
142. The tools for this
series were developed
at the Visible Language
Workshop by Suguru
Ishizaki. Series developed
by Muriel Cooper, 1988.

I-6.

Visual Language Workshop.
Anti-aliased type. An early,
experimental resolution to
a problem still confronting
graphic design. Developed
by the Media Laboratory
in 1972.

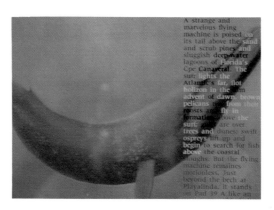

I-7.

Visual Language Workshop.
Smart typography. In this
demonstration, type
automatically becomes
white on a dark
background and black
on a lighter ground. The
resulting improvement in
legibility is achieved to
much greater effect in
actual use.

I-8.

Visual Language Workshop.
"Perspectives." In this
example, the constraints of
a computerized grid system
are visualized. The system
accepts the parameters
established by an expert
graphic designer and then
creates options. Developed
by Ron MacNeil, the
software is an antecedent
to today's desktop
publishing templates.

ent medium from any that we have ever known" (Heller 1989, 99). Holographic visualization, dynamic interactivity, nonsequential imagery, computer paint and animation systems, artificial intelligence programming, and a seamless multimedia environment are among the technologies that have been and will continue to be developed at the Visible Language Workshop.

There are no typical products of the Media Laboratory. A survey of graphic imagery created by team members, however, does provide some understanding. The work often previews options available to the design community several years later. An early project exploring real-time imaging was reproduced as the cover of *Design Quarterly* 142 in 1989. Nine images explore the possibilities for interactive change. As a reader browses through options of size, placement, color and translucency, the image frame changes. Designed by Muriel Cooper, this particular series explores a variety of informational potentialities available to a reader/graphic designer confronted with seven design elements—three text segments and four images. The computer image, unlike those produced by traditional paper media, is nonpermanent. The software, developed by Suguru Ishizake, exploits that potential for change. The result is an opportunity for a new level of creative interaction between the viewer and the image.

Experiments in computer typography at the Media Laboratory began in the early 1970s. Anti-aliased type was pioneered by the Lab in 1972. The resulting mitigation of the "jaggies" was produced by introducing gradations of gray. More recently, "smart typography" has been developed to resolve a specific problem. The goal is to improve and maintain legibility of typography set upon a multicolored or shaded field. Unlike some of the computer graphic designers that followed, Muriel Cooper and her compatriotes do not accept the facts of computer design. They work to change them. In this case, illegibility is understood to be a handicap rather than a given. A solution is proposed.

Constraints are a topic of much consideration. Ron MacNeil has developed programs that permit the professional graphic designer to create a set of guidelines within which the computer manufactures possibilities. An "expert grid system," Perspectives, is an alternative means to provide untrained desktop publishers with acceptable graphics. Rather than working as a template, Perspectives is a system of prototypes. The constraints and rules govern the construction of a grid and limit the design alternatives provided. The resulting design environment is the field in which all later problems must be resolved. New commands can be added to the system by those who are adequately equipped to do so.

Long before HyperText and hypermedia became commonplace, designers such as David Small were creating what the Workshop called the electronic book. *The Fundamentals of Color* was created in 1987 and 1988. Reader interactivity is combined with

1-9.

Visual Language Workshop. An electronic book, *Fundamentals of Color*, was created with a program developed by David Small (1987—1988). A demonstration of a dynamically interactive text combined with illustrations and translation shifts from English to German.

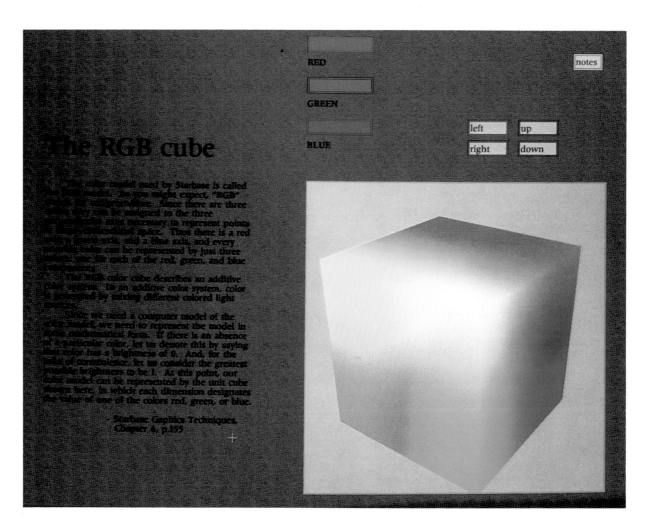

1-10.

Visual Language Workshop. Detail from a page, *Fundamentals of Color*. An annotation editor provided by the software allows the reader to make comments and save them for later review. The interactive electronic book is a predecessor of hypermedia.

translucent text and an annotation editor. Translucency refers to the ability to shift from one text language to another (in this case, from English to German). The editor permits the reader to add and edit comments, which can later be retrieved for review. The dynamics of the approach cannot be communicated in a traditional text (such as this one). The electronic book, and NewsPeek, an electronic publishing program that edits the news to suit personal tastes, are glimpses toward a possible future rapidly becoming the present. Developed under the direction of Walter Bender, NewsPeek was a predecessor of program services such as Prodigy, which now provide access via phone modem to newspaper coverage, encyclopedic information, stock and sports reports, and the like. This prototype personalized newspaper was discussed in print years before such services were available to the public (see Aldersey Williams 1987).

The actual, visual results of this research are not as significant as the impact these efforts have had on the workplace. As with any invented technique, the work of those that follow improve on first experiments.

In certain ways, however, improvements cannot be made. Researchers at the Media Laboratory have created outlooks as well as tools and techniques. Unlike many other high-tech research efforts, the Workshop and Laboratory are as interested in approach as in applications. Negroponte believes that the defining characteristic of his work is "to personalize, and thus humanize, computers and their relationships with the mass media" (Cooper 1989, 19). The success of that effort is not as noticeable as the very visible results of new technologies. This comparative invisibility, however, is not a reflection of any insignificance. The crucial contribution of the Workshop has been to "make humane" the computer environment. These efforts are continuing. Computer designers are fortunate that such an effort has been made on their behalf.

Most graphic designers are still more concerned with style and form than with content or responsibility. Distinct forms of computer graphic design have emerged. Four approaches will be discussed and documented in Chapters 2 through 5.

The dividing line among computer graphic designers is between invisibility and visibility. Computer graphic design need not look and act a certain way. Stylistic options available to users of the new tool are the new primitivism, the sophisticated design epitomized by April Greiman, an invisible computer graphic design that appears fundamentally similar to "traditional" design, and a new entry—a sophisticated style featuring pages that do not overly appear to be computed but that can be achieved only through the use of the computer. There are, then, two visible and two invisible computer design styles.

The new primitivism was formed in the same cultural reactor as the American and British forms of Punk. This low-tech alternative celebrates the pixelated forms and digitized patterns of early computer imagery. Independence from the traditional is visually declared.

Sharing this revolutionary spirit, the new sophisticates agree with the new primitives that the medium is indeed the message. Increased computer power and a new aesthetic sensibility seem to require these designers to explore possibility. Designers who emulate the careful and courageous explorations of April Greiman have created a high-tech ethos marked by a look quite dissimilar to primitivism but obviously computerized.

Most of us have been influenced by, but have not assisted in, the creation of visible computer alternatives. The majority of people who use the computer use the computer invisibly, with little or no effect on style. Invisible computer graphic designers are divided into two camps. Many (perhaps most) have found themselves able to move from traditional media to the computer with little difficulty. The tool changes without visible notice. For these designers, a primary reason to use the new technology is the contraction of computer time.

A second large group has combined an aversion to pixels with an interest in contemporary form. Graphic designers such as Michael Weymouth and Nancy Skolos, and industrial design firms such as frogdesign, have actively participated in the creation of a new aesthetic. Denying the explicit language of visible computer graphics, these designers have nevertheless created a new visual language. Many of their images could not have been created without the computer. They do not, however, maintain an easy allegiance to the medium. Attempting to explore and create without passionate acceptance of readily available visual phrases, the newest computer designers extend limits rather than accept them.

These four stylistic categories characterize ways in which the computer may be used. They are not mutually exclusive. Many

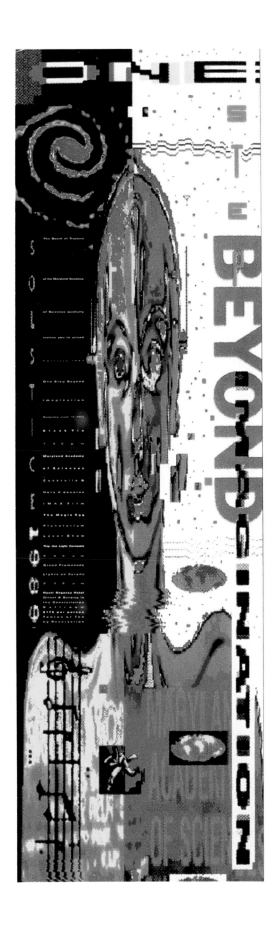

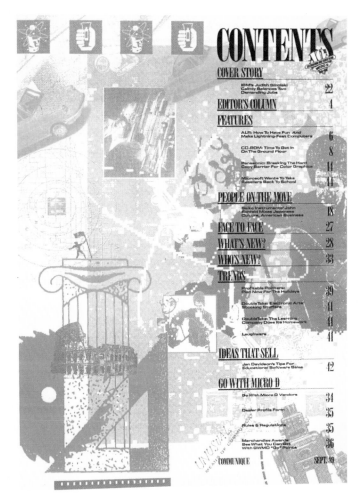

1–11.

New Primitivism. Tim Thompson. Poster
for Maryland Academy of Sciences,
Baltimore, Maryland. Developed for
a fundraiser, "One Step Beyond
Imagination," using the Lightspeed Page
Layout System 20 computer graphics
system with output on laser ink-jet printer
(left).

1–12.

New Sophisticates: the cultured computer.
Ingram Micro D Design, Santa Ana,
California. Illustrated by Johnee Bee. The
Contents page for *Communique* magazine
was created using Aldus PageMaker and
Abaton C-Scan software run on the Apple
Macintosh II. Typography and other design
elements are layered in a postmodernist
strategy common by 1989 (above).

1-13.
Invisible I. Burns, Connacher & Waldron, New York. Robert Burns, designer; Michael Crumpton, illustrator. Poster: "There's A Cancer Threatening Our Parks and Public Lands." 1989. A set of four posters for the National Park Service was commissioned by Vincent Gleason, head of publications at the U.S. Department of the Interior. The purpose: to increase public awareness of the problem of drug use in the national park system. The posters were created with Adobe Illustrator II and Aldus PageMaker on the Apple Macintosh II. The series has not been visually effected by the use of computer as medium, owing more to the visual examples of Bradbury Thompson, Paul Rand, and Milton Glaser than to the work of other computer designers. There is an obvious effect, however, on the ability to complete the project within a four-day deadline.

1-14.
Invisible II. Bert Monroy, Brooklyn, New York. Dave's 5 & 10. Artificial realities are produced without visible relationship to the computer. This illustration was not scanned; the entire work is drawn with Adobe Illustrator 88 and PixelPaint. Color blending is achieved through PixelPaint. Created with the Apple Macintosh II, the image was output on the Montage film recorder. The experimental illustration has been published in *Verbum* and *MacWorld*.

of the best, including April Greiman, the most significant graphic designer of this first generation, have used the computer to create in each of the styles at different times. Some graphic designers limit themselves to a particular meta-style. Others move from one to the other and back again. Creativity often creates problems for critics who insist on placing designers into particular places.

Admitting that difficulty, these four descriptors are a pragmatic means to divide and discuss contemporary messages. As with any other description of a contemporary event, there is the real risk of looking foolish in hindsight. The technology we are examining is developing at an increasingly rapid pace. From our vantage point in the early 1990s, it is impossible to predict what will be possible even in a few years. By 2000, the year of the new millennium, several new revolutions may have occurred. Revolutions may be forecast. They cannot really be understood before they occur.

These divisions are both real and useful. They are not settled. Contemporary graphic designers may not conveniently continue to place themselves into these specific categories. If, as expected, they do not, they nevertheless must react to the premier computer designers now working. Irrespective of the system in which that work is categorized, this is the genesis. The beginning of all that follows will be found here.

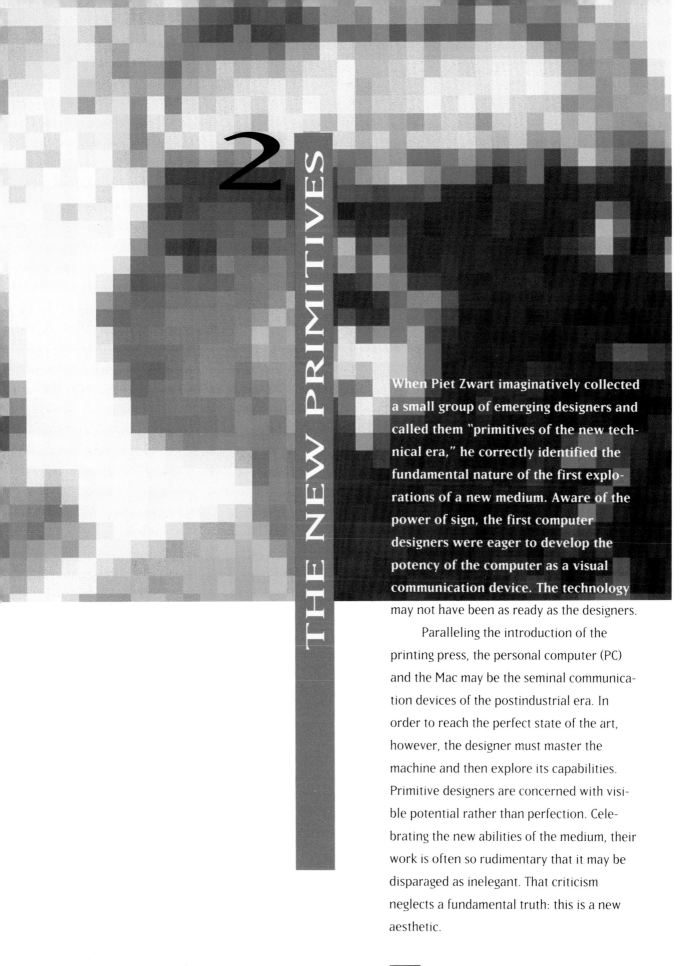

2

THE NEW PRIMITIVES

When Piet Zwart imaginatively collected a small group of emerging designers and called them "primitives of the new technical era," he correctly identified the fundamental nature of the first explorations of a new medium. Aware of the power of sign, the first computer designers were eager to develop the potency of the computer as a visual communication device. The technology may not have been as ready as the designers.

Paralleling the introduction of the printing press, the personal computer (PC) and the Mac may be the seminal communication devices of the postindustrial era. In order to reach the perfect state of the art, however, the designer must master the machine and then explore its capabilities. Primitive designers are concerned with visible potential rather than perfection. Celebrating the new abilities of the medium, their work is often so rudimentary that it may be disparaged as inelegant. That criticism neglects a fundamental truth: this is a new aesthetic.

The visual climate created by the computer was largely unknown in 1980. Throughout the eighties, the pixel was increasingly manipulated to create new models of appropriateness and beauty. The primitives argued, both verbally and visually, that this utterly contemporaneous media permitted, and even required, a new mannerism. Often idiosyncratic and affected, their heavily pixelated, low-tech articulation became a declaration by the mid-1980s. The question was asked, Did these designers create in this way because they didn't know any better? The answer: yes. New primitives did not know any better because they were self-proclaimed experts creating a new aesthetic style. They therefore knew best what they were doing. They succeeded in announcing a new language.

Messages were (and continue to be) visually low-tech for two reasons. First, design intent may exceed technological capability. Designers can, at times, do no better than produce visual proclamations which seem infused with crudities when judged by the precepts of the past. John Hersey, the Thunder Jockeys, and Rudy VanderLans continue to accept this "vulgarity," even revel in it, because they argue that old standards are no longer legitimate. Second, in their search with other postmodernists for a new visual order, many primitives accept technology on its own terms. Computer designers are both computer artists and professional communicators. In selecting between the media and the message, they vote in favor of the medium rather than the visual expectation of an audience. They are resolved to produce work that explicitly looks like it was produced by a computer. Coarse bitmaps and pixels are the tribal tattoos of a new visual order. Extreme visibility is an affirmation of both the machine and the new machine aesthetic.

If the computer is the driving engine of the postindustrial age, the new primitives offer alternative design/lifestyles created with that engine. As technology improved, most accepted what they were given. The intent, however, is a constant. The new primitives explore the intrinsic possibilities of the computer as a computer, not as a traditional design device. This is an inherently revolutionary form. The computer is not just a replacement for the T-square. It eradicates *all* the old order—both the tool and the manner of the tool.

PRIMITIVE PURPOSES

We cannot know the purposes of the artists of Lascaux, of Altamira, and of La Magdelaine. Given that history is something we cannot know, but can only honestly conclude, the inevitable arguments for historical relativism can be made. Perhaps the best we can hope for is intelligent interpretation. Unfortunately, we may be no better off in judging the explicitly subjective postmodern message.

Contemporary discoverers of the computer are primitive for two different reasons and thereby accomplish two different purposes. Aesthetically, their work is a rejection of the elegance of Swiss internationalism. To criticize the work for what it does not hope to be, for not meeting modernist standards of clarity, is a fundamentally flawed (and critically unfair) approach. A new design strategy should not be interpreted in the old clothes of dated vocabulary and past expectations. Epistemically, the primitives search for tribal meaning, the same sort of message evoked in the postmodernism of Wolfgang Weingart and in the magazines and album covers of the Punk designer. Tapping into the currency of contemporary vision, these designers are attempting to create new paradigms.

The motivations of the contemporary designer are often as unclear as those of "older" primitives. In carving out understanding in a subjective universe, it is doubly inappropriate to believe that we can immediately accept as true (or even accurate) the designer's own words. We may misinterpret the designer's motives; we may also be faced with the possibility that verbal expectations do not match visual results. Fortunately, several designers have been open in declaring their intentions. At the very least, these manifestos provide a starting point from which an understanding can be forged.

Often misunderstood, several designers have assigned themselves the difficult task of charting this new territory. In the United States, Japan, and Britain, influential models have impacted the mainstream. The discussion of this work is an account of influence. The real measure of the success of the new primitivism, however, is not contemporary influence. When we draw as children, without the "advantages" gained through the mastery of technique, we are primitives, untaught yet pure. Whether in the history of art or the history of the child, what we discover we retain. As Swarte understood, to call art "primitive" is not a disparagement. Primitivism is the first, necessary, and indispensable step toward a still unknown future.

Rudy VanderLans is the art director of Emigre Graphics, a studio established in 1984 in Berkeley, California. A native of the Netherlands, VanderLans co-founded the firm with the type designer Zuzana Licko, whose work will be discussed in Chapter 6. From its inception, one of the purposes of the studio has been to provide computer design prototypes. *Emigre* magazine is an exemplary representative of the missionary aspect of new primitivism. Because the magazine is a visual manifesto specifically aimed at the graphic designer, relatively few copies of the magazine are sold (recent press runs have exceeded the 2000 copies of the first few issues). Other studios and magazines have been influenced by the "Magazine That Ignores Boundaries," but the intellectual purity of the original is dissipated by copyists. As with the work of Neville Brody, The Duffy Design Group, and any other original designer, innovation is based on intelligent decision making and design sense. Unintelligent design clones, meanwhile, are only vaguely aware of the good that they steal.

VanderLans is not angered by the popularization of his methods or mannerisms. In an unusual turnabout, he is actually pleased: *Emigre* is created with the acknowledgment (and, perhaps, even hope) that it will be plagiarized. His magazine is a forum for exploration. When ideas are appropriated by others, the forum is successful. VanderLans states: "Designers exploring the technologies of today's revolutionary computer age are creating visual forms that will serve as prece-

dent for future design" (*ID* 1988, 58). The pages of *Emigre* are explicit models to be followed. These patterns, moreover, are constitutionally declared to be new: "Computer technology has advanced the state of graphic art by such a quantum leap into the future that it has brought the designer back to the most primitive of graphic ideas and methods. It's no wonder that our first computer art usually resembles that of naive cave paintings! This return to our primeval ideas allows us to reconsider the basic assumptions made in the creative design process . . . we are faced with evaluating the basic rules of design that we formerly took for granted" (*Emigre II*:1).

Accepting the "computer look" of low-end machines, VanderLans believes it is in the computer designer's (meaning, in the near future, every designer's) best interest to deal with the original values of technology. Comparing bitmaps with the texture of oils, he argues that computer imagery is no more visually intrusive than are airbrush, calligraphy, or paint. Computer imaging is now understood as a more radical, perhaps freer, form of expression only because of its unfamiliarity. The "radical" nature of computer-aided design is a matter of perception rather than fact. One of the founding principles of *Emigre* is to dispel the obscurity of the machine. When the designs created by Emigre Graphics are replicated by others, the act of duplication is a procreation of style. VanderLans understands the profane necessity of proliferation by counterfeit.

2-1.

Rudy VanderLans. Cover of
Emigre 12: Press Time!,
published in 1989. The
layering strategy of *Emigre*
is evident. An example of
VanderLans's contention
that the contemporary
computer graphic designer
need not be concerned
with traditional beliefs
regarding legibility. The
emphasis is on visual
communication rather
than verbal identification
with the past.

Although the products of new primitivism are indeed new, they are not artificial. Originality is necessary because, and not simply by virtue of, a reaction to the new media: "creating a graphic language with today's tools will mean forgetting the styles of archaic technologies" (*Emigre 11*:1). Although *Emigre* is not always successful in forging a new graphic language, the attempt is an honest one. There are several vocabularies at work. In his cover for *Emigre 12*, in each page of *Emigre 8*, and in dozens of other examples, VanderLans explores the value of the computer as a typographic layering device. Several lines of type are gathered together, overlapped, and intertwined. The resulting weave of verbal confusion is a debate between objectivity and the future. The subjectivity of postmodernism nearly always wins. We understand, first visually and then intellectually, that this is indeed a new form of communication. The weaving is both verbal and visual, creating intuitive effects supported by appropriate imagery. In a poster, we are confronted with fragments of words, pixelated photographs, vibrant colors, palm trees, and fingerprints. What do these images mean? As the logical positivist philosopher Ludwig Wittgenstein remarked (and April Greiman remembered), they mean what we make them mean. It makes sense when we give it sense.

Humor and mystery are integral parts of the Emigre arsenal. Lexigraphic explanations that do not explain are sprinkled about the magazine: "Do you read me?", "The new and improved Emigre," "Warning: Contents may

2-2.
Rudy VanderLans. Page from *Emigre 8: Alienation*, 1988. In this case, both legibility and visibility of the purely typographic message is sacrificed. Each issue of *Emigre* is descriptively titled to indicate either theme or content.

2-3.
Rudy VanderLans. Poster exhibiting the postmodern penchant for seemingly random images swimming about the page. Here, the ubiquitous fingerprint, a line drawing reminiscent of the 1950s, polaroids, and the palm tree combine to intimate hidden significances. 1989.

EMIGRE N

é·mi·gré (em'ə grā')

Design Features: Graceful, festive, tropical feeling
Luxuriant vacation mood. Strong vertical. Dramatic,
especially in groups. Jungle feeling when used with
such plants as bamboo. Eventual skyline silhouette.

sit

Design Features: Graceful, festive, tr
Luxuriant vacation mood. Strong verti
especially in groups. Jungle feeling
such plants as bamboo. Eventual s

be offensive to some," and "Do not try this in your home." Foreign language inscriptions and experiments in letterform are common. These typographic signatures operate on the same level as urban graffiti: though as sophisticates we may not know what they mean, we know that they do have meaning. And we personally appreciate that understanding.

The emotional and personal impact afforded by computer design is not the exclusive territory of Rudy VanderLans. He is certainly its master. Even in occasional pieces produced by and for the studio, craftsman-like care is taken in the preparation of the visual sign. In the postindustrial age, we may not be able to know the signified, but the visual sign remains a product of craft. VanderLans accepts the autocracy of the universal design principles of comprehensibility, communication, and expression. The task of the computer designer is to accomplish those goals within the limits established by technology and the fundamentals of design and design practice. His pages often appear to go beyond those bounds. He argues that such a conclusion is a function of our own unfamiliarity with the medium.

Our perceptions of computer design are regulated by our familiarity with tradition. As new primitivism becomes more pedestrian, visually literate individuals will be better able to judge its values. In the 1990s, *Emigre* visions filtered into the mediascape of advertising, television, and print journalism. The creative authenticity of VanderLans pages will be inevitably diluted in this mainstream-

Emigre 11 Design and production: **Rudy VanderLans.** Editorial consultant: **Alice Polesky.** Emigre #11 was designed and produced on a Macintosh Plus using ReadySetGo! for page layouts. All typefaces were originally designed for Emigre magazine by **Zuzana Licko** using Fontographer. Distribution & Promotion: **Patrick Li.** Printing: **Lompa Printing.** X-tra special thanks: Apple Computer, Inc., Bitstream Inc., Letraset USA, Optronics, Lompa Printing, Willem Kars, Peter van Merriënboer, Paul Stoute, Verbum. The page numbers in this issue were designed by the graduate design students at California Institute of the Arts, Valencia CalArts 1 Somi Kim. 2 John Calvelli. 3 Johanna Jacob. 4 Barry Deck. 5 Kali Nikitas. 6 Wolfgang Blueggel. 7 Mohd. Raziff Alias. 8 Dennis Sopczynski. 9 Patricia Osborn. 0 Barbara Glauber. A Robin Cottle. B C. LaRou. Macintosh and LaserWriter are trademarks of Apple Computer, Inc. PostScript is a trademark of Adobe Systems, Inc. Fontographer is a trademark of Altsys Corporation. ReadySetGo! is a trademark of Manhattan Graphics Corporation.

KEEP ON READING

2-4.

Rudy VanderLans. Details of Contents page, *Emigre II: Macintosh Design.* The typefaces used in *Emigre* are most often designed by Zuzana Licko, discussed in Chapter 6. *Emigre* interviews are an important source of information regarding the typographic and design avant garde.

and I got a half inch head trim on the film that is prou:
: mean I have to guillotine cut, or do you want me to ta
tuff ... *RICK*: No, we want everything with a half inch
ard, line one!) trim, even if you have to
out. *ELIZABETH*: OK that's fine. *RICK*: Then we should la'
 out and get proper lip from front to back. *ELIZABETH*: N
eh **(Richaaaard, line one!)**
e trim on the folder? *RICK*: Let's see. It's eleven and a '
s twentytwo and a half, out of twentyfive, that's two a
s split between front and back. If you want one and or
. *ELIZABETH*: Can you run that through the müller? *RICK*
 I thought it was one and one eighth. *RICK*: We'll have
 that. How about this letterpress insert? We can run thi
 müller without a problem. We'll put the cover on ... or is
e should marry these two inside signatures first and t
n. We can combine it **(Richaaaard, line**
 piece. Actually it depends on what that letterpress pi
RUDY: It's printed on a ten by thirteen inch sheet. They
and a half inch flap and it will be die cut in the shape c

2-5.
Rudy VanderLans.
Experimental typography.
Interior front cover of
Emigre 12: Press Time!.
The grouping of different
typefaces in different sizes
and weights is a favorite
device which has now
reached the mainstream.

2-6.
Rudy VanderLans.
Experimental typography
in *Emigre 18: Type-Site*,
1991.

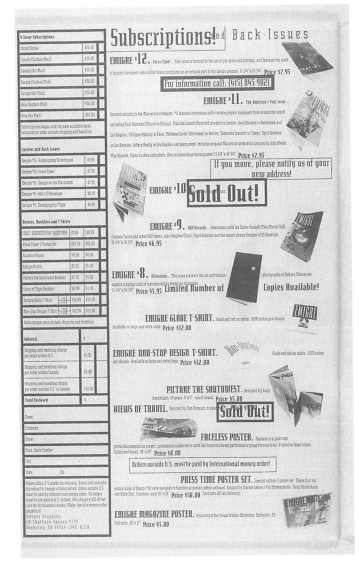

2-7.
Rudy VanderLans.
Broadside advertising the
forthcoming publication
of *Emigre 13: Redesigning
Stereotypes*, Spring 1990
(above left).

2-8.
Rudy VanderLans. Back
issues order form.
Published both as an
independent folder and as
the last page of *Emigre 13:
Redesigning Stereotypes*,
Spring 1990 (left).

2-9.
Rudy VanderLans. Detail,
cover of *Glashaus*,
Summer 1987. A
commercial version of
Emigre retaining much of
the original approach. The
new magazine has been
described as *Emigre* with
advertising (above right).

ing process. However, the ideas of computer graphic designers featured in *Emigre*—Wolfgang Weingart, Rick Valicenti, Max Kisman, April Greiman, Hans-Rudolf Lutz, Hamish Stuart, and Warren Lehrer among them— have been seen and appropriated. Multidimensional layout, bold computer graphics, and intuitive technology have been commandeered by other publication designers.

As a design studio, Emigre Graphics is a rarity: the copying of its forms has assured aesthetic and commercial success. Clients have included Apple Computer, Adobe Systems, and the University of California. Several new magazines, including *Shift* and *Glashaus,* have helped to shift the studio's focus from experimental publication design to the difficult task of integrating advertising with tech-expressionist text. As in its earliest efforts, Emigre Graphics will continue to assume responsibility for the education of the computer design illiterates among us.

Illustration software written for desktop was the greatest impetus for the use of the computer as an illustration tool. Experimentation, however, began before 1985. John Hersey was among the first to create both interesting images and lasting standards for computer illustration excellence. Born in Calgary, Alberta, Hersey attended the Art Center College of Design (Pasadena) and began an illustration career in Vancouver in 1982. He has mastered a variety of media which he continues to use. Watercolors, oil paints, pen and ink, and colored pencil have not been completely replaced by new technology.

Hersey's attachment to the computer was fostered by *MacWorld Magazine* and an Apple Macintosh in 1983. Moving his office to San Francisco, he began the explorations that were to develop into an often-copied aesthetic. This is a new species of illustration: textural effects, chromatic manipulations owing much to the California Style, and by-products of the Macintosh screen coalesce into a specific, individual, and easily recognizable computer design vocabulary.

By 1987, Hersey's client list included an interesting mix of computer magazines, California New Wave proponents, and Fortune 500 corporations. *PC World, Mac World, Byte,* and *Personal Computing* had been joined by American Telephone and Telegraph (AT&T), Apple Computer and mainstream design offices, including Pentagram. The addition of clients such as Esprit, Benetton, and Paper Moon Graphics reflected Hersey's interest in Californian style.

The vivid pastels, easygoing manner, and offhanded sophistication were both marketing strategies and a genuine sense of place. Almost alone among computer illustrators, Hersey managed, in his early work, to harness that aesthetic within the machine. The distinguished architecture of Michael Manwaring, Sussman/Prezja, and Michael Vanderbyl was remarkably transmuted into a heavily pixelated form that was still appropriate. The task was made all the more difficult because of Hersey's interest in the expressionist choppiness of Punk and New Wave stylists. Reflecting the eclecticism of the age and the area in which he worked, Hersey recombined New Wave, Punk, California Style, and the computer. The merger of such an awkward potpourri of influences necessarily resulted in something immediately new. A host of designers and illustrators quickly followed the pattern.

Confronted by a parasitic secondary wave, the courage of the original is often difficult to see and appreciate. Lost in a wave of imitation, significant work can be neglected, even disparaged. Doggedly adopting the pixels inherent in the Macintosh screen, Hersey has consistently developed his own vocabulary. An important early example is his cover for *Pacific Wave: California Graphic Design,* a catalog of an exhibition at the Museo Fortuny in Venice, Italy, in 1987. Sponsored by the Centro di Documentazione di Palazzo Fortuny, the exhibition featured the work of over twenty California graphic designers who had already affected graphic design through-

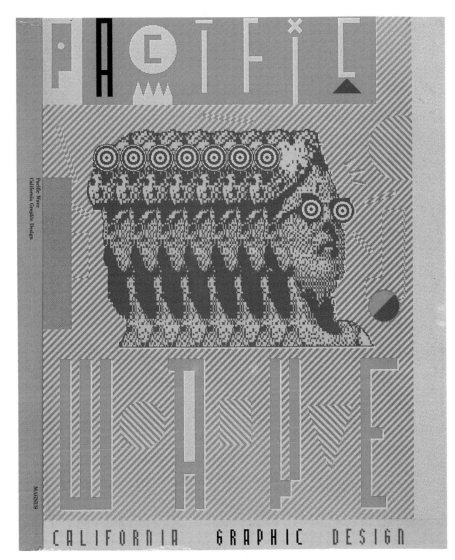

2-10.

John Hersey. Cover
illustration. *Pacific Wave:
California Graphic Design*.
Udine, Italy: Magnus
Edizioni, 1987. Type
was generated as an
illustration on the Apple
Macintosh.

2-11.

John Hersey.
Computerized portrait of
Yul Brynner for *Emigre*
magazine, 1988.

out the world. The cover is a wicked collection of New Wave conceits, California color, Hersey contributions to the new vocabulary, and pixelation. A repeated human figure dominates a frame of nontraditional typographic forms related to the experiments of Neville Brody and the British Punk movement. Dizzying patterns of diagonal line, confusing geometric forms, and abrupt chromatic changes challenge us.

The two interior spreads given over to Hersey's work are typical of his use of repeated patterns to create a dialogue of competing visual frames. The stylization is obviously artificial. There is no connection to a real world. These primitive exploitations of technology do not connect to the viewer or the world in which the viewer exists. In detail, the illustration seems to consist of a random collection of computer doodles. Perhaps they are. But they do contribute to a whole. The viewer cannot ignore this work; even if the first attempt to create meaning is unsuccessful, one wanders about the page with a curious combination of wonder, doubt, and amusement.

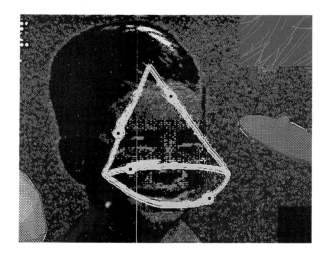

Hersey's work can be criticized. It should not be criticized on the grounds established by other, radically different design aesthetics. Lack of legibility and clear-headed meaning may be disruptive. It is not irresponsible. Primitive computer graphic design must be recognized for what it is rather than be criticized for what it is not. Neville Brody has made this point regarding his own work: "If you break down a tradi-

2-12.

John Hersey. Repetitive design from *Pacific Wave*, 1987. A pair of two-page spread illustrations were published as representative samples of his work (opposite, top).

2-13.

John Hersey. A second spread from *Pacific Wave*, 1987. A child's smiling face is digitized together with dot patterns, geometric shapes, a flying saucer, and mysterious design elements (opposite, bottom).

2-14.

John Hersey. Illustration typical of Hersey's "visual junk" style. Digitized objects and drawings populate a space that becomes a lively circus of visual delights. The allusional space is related to the work of European and American Post-Modernists who count on the determinant effort of the viewer.

2-15.

John Hersey. Computer illustration exemplifying Hersey's efforts to create realities that are mythical rather than virtual. Although still markedly primitive in style, the later work achieves a greater depth of intellectual layering. Unlike earlier pieces which depend purely on revolutionary style as a marker for meaning, the attitude of recent illustrations is more allusive. Like Greiman, Hersey has gone deeper in his search for a personal statement.

2-16.

John Hersey. "Ecology." An illustration commissioned for a series regarding health concerns and the wellness movement. On the back is a quote from Dr. Jonathan Miller: "We contain an internal world which is just as active and complicated as the one we live in."

tional structure, it can go in one of several ways. It can be flat and boring. It can alienate through its jarring with what is normally accepted. Or it can actually entice attention" (Labuz 1991, 69). A continuing, permanent problem in viewing any new work is to determine standards by which the work may be judged. If the criteria are to include originality and the degree to which secondary work is based on that originality, Hersey's work is among the most significant of the first period of computer graphic illustration.

Not all of this work is problematic. Hersey's portrait of Yul Brynner as the robot sheriff in the futuristic film *Westworld,* for example, is drawn in the recognizably choppy style of primitivism. But here the angular, postmodern mask is quite understandable. A mechanistic image inspires visions of a disquieting potential future. The textural effects are the same as those used in earlier experimental efforts. Hersey's working technique combines the traditional and the technologically unusual. In these days of light pens and bit pads, he uses the pencil and the mouse as his drawing instruments: "I always pre-sketch everything, but I don't enter it by tracing on a graphics tablet. I've gotten so fast with the mouse that I don't need to" (Fulton 1989, 96). All of his computer drawings are completed with the mouse.

In his recent work, Hersey has continued to adapt his experimental style in an attempt to achieve a more direct, increasingly immediate communication. He continues to illustrate for computer magazines.

2-17.
John Hersey. Computer illustration for article in *MacWorld,* "Crashed Disk Rescue." Readers are advised about methods to rescue a crashed hard disk. Art director: Joanne Hoffman.

2-18.
John Hersey. Fabric patterns for Esprit, used in the Spring '87 line. Hersey repeats symbols for sports clubs imagined by Michael Mabry, James Nevins, and himself. Left to right: yachting/bowling, mountaineering/golf, sumo wrestling/tennis.

Other projects have, however, included the commercially mainstream: illustrations for greeting cards, fabric designs, and advertising. The results are no less interesting. Like VanderLans, Hersey continues to challenge boundaries and the viewer. His recent success is completely understandable. As his experiments achieve results, we recognize their value. We are certainly not yet complacent.

Visual challenges of a primitive order did not and do not emanate solely from Southern California. Malcolm Garrett, Terry Jones, Peter Saville, and Neville Brody supplied much of the early aesthetic fuel required to incorporate an industrialized primitive approach in Great Britain. Cheap spontaneity, a neo-Dada abandonment of conventionality, and a "decay through process" undercurrent were necessary preconditions for the creation of a new visual order. Nihilistic Punk, though visually related to computer primitivism, was an entirely different cultural response. Punk· was a rejection of the past, the present, and the future. The new primitives accepted, even congratulated, the future.

There are many reasons for the profound differences between concurrent and overlapping aesthetics. The contrast in economic conditions between Britain and California in the late 1970s and early 1980s was remarkable. Michael Vanderbyl understood the fortunate position of those graphic designers connected to the Silicon Valley and the media center of Los Angeles at the beginning of the information age. "California has a unique client base, because many of the companies didn't exist ten to fifteen years ago (such as the high technology companies). . . . This may account for their receptiveness to more progressive ideas. It takes good clients to make good design" (Camuffo 1987, 15). In Great Britain, meanwhile, persistent labor strikes, high unemployment, ravaging inflation, and social stratification forged a

different response to a very different culture. Punk designers did not have good clients. They had no clients at all. The wine label and corporate identity of the California designer was replaced by a poorly mimeographed British magazine freely distributed and designed to be thrown away.

California designers were located within an experimental, rising cultural tide—the Pacific Wave—that impressed, and continues to impress, the rest of America, and much of the world. British designers were faced with a pessimistic ragout of violence in Northern Ireland, a recognition of decay, and widespread insecurity. Economically and culturally, Britain and the rest of the world were a different place than California. Many designers, including April Greiman, Lucille Tenazas, Rudy VanderLans, and John Hersey, understood and emigrated westward.

For primitive computer designers, however, the most significant advantage California could offer was obvious: California had the computers. During the experimental phase of the new primitivism, computers were not ubiquitous. A Punk designer working in Britain in the early 1980s had no access to the technology being created in the Silicon Valley. California designers had the first important impact on computer graphic design in part because they could use technology when other designers could not.

This is not to say that the new primitivism is restricted to the pastels of the various incarnations of New Wave, Pacific Wave,

2-19.

Vorm Vijf. Self-promotional poster for
design group based in The Hague. 1984. The
heavily pixelated imagery reflects the best
possibility available to computer graphic
designers at the time of production. The
resulting sense of anomie meshes well with
the burgeoning European Postmodernist
aesthetic of the time.

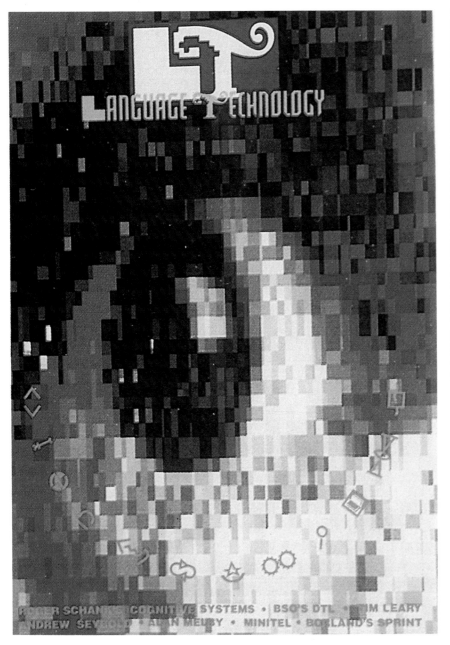

2-20.

Max Kisman. Cover of *Language Technology*. Low-resolution color bitmaps are used to maximum chromatic and visual effect. The Amiga was used to color black and white images digitized through a video scanner. Typefaces and typographic layout were created with the Apple Macintosh.

Mo, just give me a basic system hardcore supporters and zealots could such information be supplied Have you ever wondered what it would original television technology Something I've already done like this almost as much as I like I want to hook up my I'm also wondering if I can do Soon you will be to create Leading-edge I was shocked when I opened my Even if you've never been when I saw a full-page photo after I'd carefully read it needs a lot of care and the same concern I have I drew from the e+perience

2-21.

Max Kisman. Page design reproduced in *Emigre II: Macintosh Design*. VanderLans comments: "Six designers were invited to each create one page with the Macintosh. The pages were placed throughout this issue to provide the reader with a little encouragement to 'Keep on Reading.' " VanderLans's interest in the issue of reading was echoed in the title of *Emigre 15: do you read me?* The topic has also been taken up by 8vo. In this page, Kisman reflects on his own European/Bauhaus/ de Stijl/modernist heritage. Twisted, universal icons of reading are ironically combined with typography most difficult to read. As with other primitives, the emphasis is on visual form as opposed to verbal explication—the revolutionary opposite of Swiss modernism.

or California Style. After the early 1980s, important contributions were made possible by the growing democratization of the technology.

Vorm Vijf (Form Five) was one of the first Dutch design groups to use computer technology. The visual obscurity of a 1984 image is related to the European Postmodernism of Wolfgang Weingart, Grapus, and Roman Cieslewicz. In a definitive break from the clarity of de Stijl, overlapping illegibility of white, red, and black typography and digitally impersonalized figures are combined. The self-promotional poster joins a Dutch avant garde graced by the work of Studio Dumbar, Jan Van Toorn, Hard Werken, and Ko Sliggers. The strategy of layering typography and imagery is commandeered, as is the emphasis on depersonalization. Based in The Hague, Vorm Vijf continues the effort to computerize the Dutch design environment. Max Kisman, a computer graphic designer from Amsterdam, has contributed to Dutch New Primitivism and the development of the worldwide aesthetic. His covers for *Language Technology* are exemplary samples of coarse bitmap technology. Using both the Amiga and the Apple, Kisman's emphasis on digitized video images have became standard within the primitive language. As with the other designers in the vanguard, he recognizes the risks of repetition: "My responsibilities as a graphic designer don't lie in repeating myself,

and I felt that with the computer, this had started happening. . . . Day after day, I was sitting behind this screen and it was getting to be a routine." (*Emigre II*, 29). Joining dozens of significant designers who have worked with VanderLans, Kisman's work for *Emigre* reflects a more recent development toward typographic experimentation. His beliefs regarding the computer as a tool represent a maturing of attitude. Acknowledging that aesthetic defects are implicit in *this* generation of computer technology, he argues that the machine must always be subservient to the designer's needs. A love/hate relationship with technology is not atypical for the experienced computer graphic designer: "Personal expression lies beyond the tools or techniques that you use, or at least it should. The computer has become one of the many tools that I use to express my ideas . . . I can't imagine life without computers anymore, even if they are not always dear to me" (*Emigre II*, 29).

As in France and in many other parts of the world, the computer has not yet had a major influence on the design vocabulary of Britain. Many firms surfaced from the firestorm of Punk and the economic revival of the early 1980s. The work of 8vo, discussed in Chapter 5, is archetypal of an objective approach popular in Great Britain. Technology is used. The theoretical perspective, however, is not based in that technology.

Thunder Jockeys is another question altogether. John England and Graham Elliot, the two principals of the firm, are not graphic designers in the traditional sense. They are not traditional in any sense. A combination of technology, multimedia presentations, cabaret, performance art, and an absence of apparent plan provides Thunder Jockeys with the opportunity to achieve their announced goal: "to disoriente ideas of constructed boringness and nicety. . . . and to to introduce optimism, loudness and color" Aldersey-Williams 1989, 53). The palette for a 1988 compact disk cover contains a dizzy amalgam of colors. Most of the 16 million colors available on the workstation manufactured by the now-defunct Artronics seem to have been used. Fittingly, the design is for the album, *Vivid,* by the rock group Living Colour. A computerized color palette occupies its appropriate place at the bottom of the image (just as it does on the Artronics screen).

A second cover done for the same group is a stunning exploration in typography. The front cover combines weird skeletal signs, a pistol, electric colors, and dramatically scattered typography spelling out the album name: Love Rears Its Ugly Head. The back cover and the compact disk itself continue these investigations into personal expressiveness with techno tools. Recalling the rejectionist mode of Dada and the expressionism of the sixties, the typography is entirely consistent with the primitive approach.

The energy of the firm is palpable even in the name the principals have chosen for themselves. Two projects the Thunder Jockeys completed in 1988 for British Satellite Broadcasting and MTV were "Thunder Jockeys in Space" and "Thunder Wear."

Computer-enhanced psychedelia, chaotic three-dimensional imagery, and apparent lack of structure are balanced by a confused, hand-drawn calligraphy that is quite human. The strategy, which has been used in fine art, in broadcast graphics, and by other graphic designers, reflects the Thunder Jockeys' insistence on the personal avenue to design. That approach is quite different from the often dispassionate graphics of John Hersey and Vorm Vijf. Whether creating video productions for MTV, perfecting their Dadaist performances, or designing rock album covers, England and Elliot emphasize the necessity of the human within the design equation. Even in a mechanistic computer environment, Thunder Jockeys uses primitivism to proclaim their own individuality.

2-22.
Thunder Jockeys. Cover of
Vivid, album and compact
disks by the rock group
Living Colour, CBS
Records, 1988. Geometric
and organic forms
compete with radical
typography and a vibrant
color selection.

2-23.
Thunder Jockeys. Detail of compact disk package, *Vivid*, CBS Records. 1988. The color palette of the Artronics work station is joined by animalistic forms.

2-24.
Thunder Jockeys. Cover of *Love Rears Its Ugly Head*, album by Living Colour, CBS Records, 1990. The typographic exploration is continued on the compact disk.

2-25.
Thunder Jockeys. Compact disk design, *Love Rears Its Ugly Head*. Album by the group Living Colour, CBS Records. The contradiction between personal expression and the light pen as medium is explored. 1990.

AFTERWORD

Irrespective of the lack of technology, the new primitivism does not seem to sprout in certain environments. In Japan, for example, computer use has understandably exploded in recent years. Yet the work of master computer designers such as Takenobu Igarashi, Kazumasa Nagai, and Mitsuo Katsui is sophisticated rather than primitive. The work, discussed in the next chapter, is visibly technological. There is little or no evidence, however, of a vocabulary similar to that created by Emigre Graphics.

What are we to make of the fact that certain design cultures, when confronted with the computer, make use of the tool in very different ways? Each designer carries the weight of the given discourse from which they have arrived. Nationality, ethnicity, environment, technology, economics, influence, and opportunity are among the factors contributing to individual decisions about how and whether to do computer graphic design. Serendipity is another, often overlooked.

If we cannot answer the question, we can at least ask it and see where the asking takes us. The new primitives have asked questions for all of us and, more than most of us, have delivered answers. Those associated with earlier design strategies may not appreciate the apparent lack of interest in legibility, in clarity, or in credible statement. The operative word is "new." The primitives are not only primitive. They are new. As such, they can be offensive. Their work has been disparaged as crude and unintelligible. Similar declarations have been made regarding many movements that were once new.

This is not an artificial avant garde. The reality of the new primitivism is apparent because it is contemporary. Manifestos of intent exist. An oeuvre has been created. Although many may wish that it not be so, this work cannot and has not been dismissed. The opposite has occurred. The cultural lag between innovation and appropriation has already started to close. The visual phrases of new primitivism are now more readily acceptable within the mainstream of graphic design, within the major periodicals, and within corporate design. Those who do appropriate might be well off to understand the meanings and intent of the original.

The semantic content inherent in an original expression is transportable. It attaches itself to the expression and carries with it the intent of the first designer. The meaning of the Esprit color system does not immediately change after it is "borrowed" by another fashion merchandiser. That is precisely why the system is pilfered—it is hoped that the same elan, the same message, is conveyed. And it is, for a time, until seemingly stolen by all. Repetition robs the expression of its first purpose.

Pixelated imagery, confused layering, and calligraphic typography carry culturally known baggage. Because these are primitive messages, the educated may require time to understand. Graphic designers copying these forms may not understand at all. These designers are on dangerous ground, taking the risk of sending wrong and inconsistent messages. They are also sadly diluting the significance of what was once new and powerful.

The imitator's lack of potency should not affect our appreciation of the vigorous archetype. As early as several years later, it requires no effort to forget and even dismiss the impact of an original, visual statement.

An alternative measure of the value of Rudy VanderLans and John Hersey is the speed at which their first paradigms have been eaten (and destroyed) by the parasitic. More significantly, they are at work creating new ones. These too will be quickly gobbled up by the copyists in our design future. Fortunately for the state of our design present, these artists have accepted the challenge of staying ahead of those less civilized than the primitives.

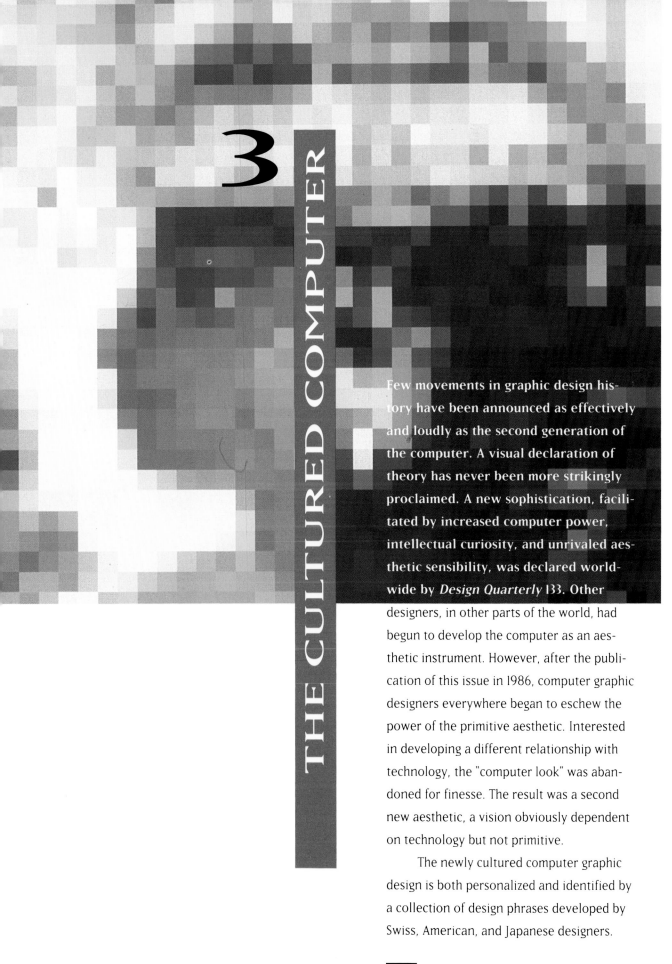

3

THE CULTURED COMPUTER

Few movements in graphic design history have been announced as effectively and loudly as the second generation of the computer. A visual declaration of theory has never been more strikingly proclaimed. A new sophistication, facilitated by increased computer power, intellectual curiosity, and unrivaled aesthetic sensibility, was declared worldwide by *Design Quarterly* 133. Other designers, in other parts of the world, had begun to develop the computer as an aesthetic instrument. However, after the publication of this issue in 1986, computer graphic designers everywhere began to eschew the power of the primitive aesthetic. Interested in developing a different relationship with technology, the "computer look" was abandoned for finesse. The result was a second new aesthetic, a vision obviously dependent on technology but not primitive.

The newly cultured computer graphic design is both personalized and identified by a collection of design phrases developed by Swiss, American, and Japanese designers.

Owing much to the technological explorations of Wolfgang Weingart at the Allgemeine Kuntsgewerbeschule in Basel, Switzerland, the initial explosion was, like the new primitivism, based in those geographic areas that offered new technology to the graphic designer. By the late 1980s, however, graphic designers outside of California and Japan had begun to adopt and develop the new aesthetic.

In Europe, before the computer, a postmodernist ethos based upon Weingartian ideas and ideals had already made significant inroads into the mannerism of the International Style. Several national styles emanated from a shared rejection of geometric clarity. Childlike illustrations, hand lettering, the use of reverse type in information bands, torn design elements, and wide letterspacing became standards. The rejection of the Swiss academy rapidly devolved, in the words of Philip Meggs, into the "New Academy." By the middle of the 1980s, New Wave was a cliche. For the computer designers that followed, the most valuable thrust of the New Wave was an emphasis on technological experimentation. Photocollage, overlaying, the photographic alteration of images, moire patterns, textural dot patterns, and the use of technical special effects were all made more readily available after the development of photocomposition and the commercial abandonment of letterpress. Weingart's development of these ideas was a first step away

from the past and toward the new technology. His intuitive visual style and his emphasis on visible intensity within an invisible order remain the cornerstone of the explorations that followed.

A second requirement of a sophisticated computer style was, of course, a technology that permitted discrimination. The development of hardware and software such as the Quantel Video and Graphics Paintboxes, the Lightspeed system, Alias Design Paint, Intelligent Light, and the Silicon Graphics workstations (to name but several) was a necessary but not sufficient cause. By the mid-1980s, it was clear to many computer experimenters that existing technology did not produce the quality required by most graphic designers. The short-term result was the development of a working method that combined traditional and computerized techniques. Many continue to pragmatically use the machine when necessary to produce a specific effect. All of the designers focused on in this chapter, however, also continue to use hand skills when required. Computer graphic design has rapidly come of age: rather than emphasize the use of technology simply for its own sake, these designers use the tool when they believe it is best to do so. There is a significant philosophical difference between the New Primitives and even newer designers. Primitives believe that "graphic" is the more significant adjective in the phrase "computer graphic design." Those that follow do not agree. The work of the second phase always appears "technological"—often more so than the work of the first Primitives. The touch of a human hand is less obvious.

In practice, this work is often created using traditional skills. The mark of the cultured computer, then, is not the necessary use of the computer. This is, rather, a graphic design style identified by visual appearance rather than computer usage. As such, it is related directly to the earlier experimentations of Weingart. April Greiman has recognized this merger of technology and tradition, coining the phrase "hybrid imagery" to refer both to her work and her working method.

For a more mature generation of computer graphic designers, the emphasis is on opportunities. When the computer can be used well, it is used. Vision is not clouded by the aesthetic in contemporary favor. These designers recognize the risk that standards of excellence will be replaced by a nihilistic aestheticism: "computer design for computer design's sake."

The enthusiasm of the first days of invention has rapidly developed into a serious attitude. "This mingling of digital image/text/page composition technology with traditional photomechanical techniques for print production" (Greiman 1990, 13) is not more conservative. If the means through which these graphic designs are created are a suitable measure, it is indeed more traditional. The experimental nature of the visual objects created is, however, unmistakable.

These results are among the most remarkable being constructed today, in any medium, by any artists. They may be among the cultural signposts of our time. Just as the work of an untrained primitive painter may be a "purer" form of expression than the recent computerized paintings of David Hockney or the earlier abstracts of Frank Stella, New Primitivism may be computer design more immaculate. Purity is not the graphic summum bonum. Visual effect, the relationship between hand and eye, and form as energy are the operational goals. Those are the benchmarks by which graphic design is tested.

The career of April Greiman has been well documented, both by contemporary chroniclers of graphic design and in her book, *Hybrid Imagery: The fusion of technology and graphic design.* Educated at the Kansas City Art Institute and the Allgemeine Kunstgewerbeschule under Armin Hoffman and Wolfgang Weingart, Greiman returned to the United States in 1971. In 1976, after teaching for several years at the Philadelphia College of Art, she decided that California was a prerequisite for her own development as a graphic designer. In *Pacific Wave*, Greiman listed hundreds of parts that make up the California whole, citing each as an influence. A short excerpt: "the strip, pacific coast highway, muscle beach, skinheads, shopping by car, zinfandel, chardonnay, ripple, wheatgrass juice, papaya shakes, chili dogs, bad coffee, counterculture, Esalen, Big Sur, Carmel, technology" (Camuffo 1987, 13). The typeset list continues for another forty lines.

Greiman's travel plans proved to be a pivotal moment in the history of recent graphic design. Transplanted, she quickly developed the technique and visual working order that became the vocabulary of the American New Wave. Accepting Weingart's belief that though it may appear to be "sometimes in a chaos . . . typography should have a hidden structure" (Weingart 1972), she captured the Day-Glo palette, varied textures, and visual choices of California to express the essence of contemporary culture. By 1982, the New Wave formula was complete. In a 1978 poster for the California Institute of the Arts, for example, more than two dozen photographic images were combined. The suggestion of a hyperspace, an infinite depth of field, became a standard phrase in the vocabulary and is still frequently borrowed. The vernacular imagery of the art school floats about the room, defying both convention and physical law. The poster is typical of Greiman's use of connotation as a means of developing messages. The hand of an invisible participant, at bottom right, creates an indefinably long foreground while the background falls into infinite clouds. Greiman's vocabulary of multiple dimensions, diagonal perspectives, wide letterspacing, overlapping visuals, and floating geometric shapes was widely copied. Eschewing the modernist technique of directed communication, her use of spatial illusion and overlapping visual elements acknowledges and requires the viewer's participation in the creation of the signified.

Criticized as both narcissistic and as visually "messy," "the queen of the New Wave" reacted by beginning the explorations that would form the basis for American Postmodernism. (Greiman, recognizing the looseness with which the term "Postmodernism" has been used, prefers the term "hybrid imagery.") In the early 1980s, two developments occurred. First, computer technology had progressed to the point that serious graphic designers began to experiment with the medium. Second, Greiman had determined the nature of her reaction to her critics: "We were getting so much resistance that

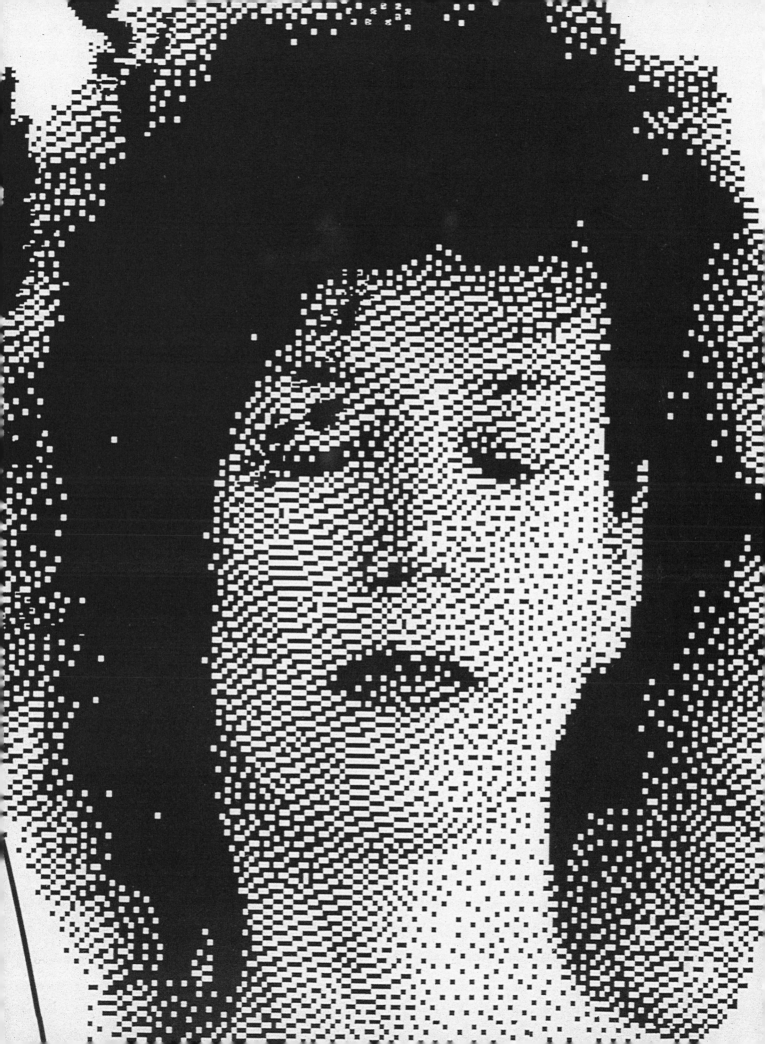

I got stubborn . . . I decided to layer in and loosen up more elements. I wanted depth and texture and surprise. It seemed to me that the human brain could sift through all that visual information and maybe enjoy it" (Hanna 1987). Determined to develop the layering technique, in 1982, Greiman discovered the computer and the video image. The synergistic result was the decision to layer information rather than images—the philosophical basis of American Postmodernism.

From 1982 through 1986, Greiman's discovery and mastery of the computer and video image led to a newer, more radical approach. Her earliest computerized work is primitive (she did much to establish the form as an independent and respected visual order). Quite quickly, however, a difference emerged. Clearly visible as technological, the second phase in the evolution of a computer aesthetic was publicly broadcast. The proclamation was actually a joint announcement. The cultured computer and American Postmodernism arrived simultaneously.

Exploring the potential of both the computer and interpretable graphics, Greiman developed her interest in the potential of computer design while teaching and serving as Director of the Visual Communications program at the California Institute of the Arts from 1982 to 1984. Her revolutionary use of digitized video input and the computerized generation of art using the Apple Macintosh culminated with the publication of *Design Quarterly* 133. Commissioned and pub-

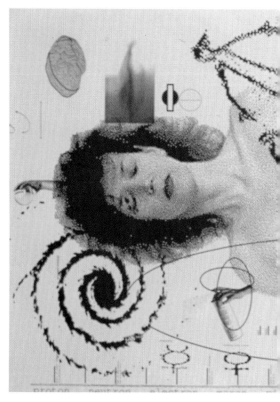

3-1.

April Greiman. *Design Quarterly* 133. Detail. 1986 (see previous page).

3-2.

April Greiman. *Design Quarterly* 133. Monotone front. The American introduction to postmodernism and the cultured computer. The self-portrait is 25½ inches by 76½ inches, folded twenty-one times to fit into a slipcase designed by Greiman. 1986 (see previous page).

3-3.

April Greiman. *Design Quarterly* 133. Back cover. Production details are joined by Zen messages, dreams, and a biography. 1986.

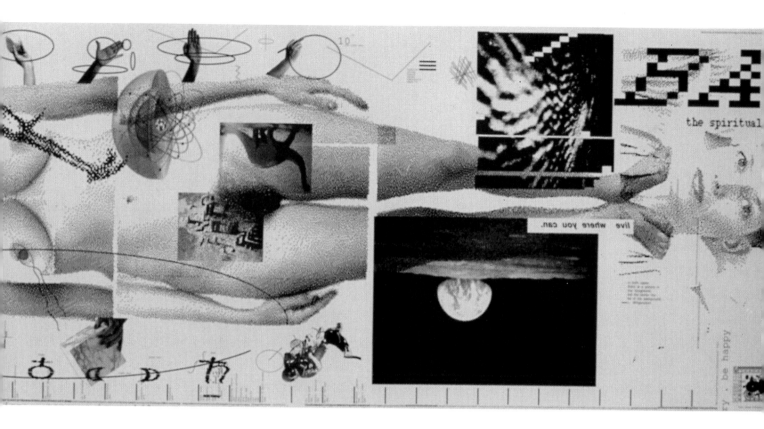

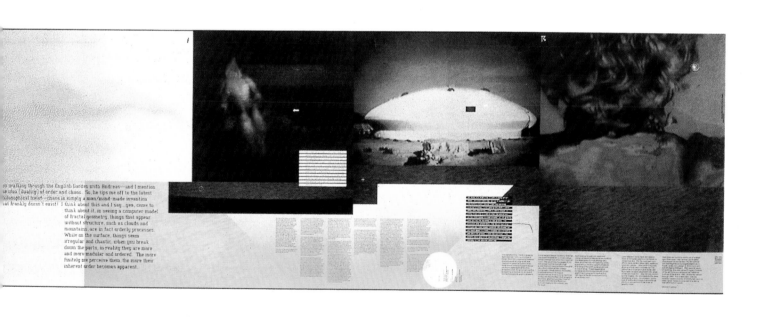

lished by the Walker Art Center of Minneapolis, the issue was intended to focus attention on the computer and on April Greiman. Given complete control of design and production by editor Mildred Friedman, Greiman certainly focused on herself. The nude self-portrait is both figurative and metaphorical. A nearly life-sized portrait is accompanied by written commentary and evocative imagery that forms, at its base, a transparent record of one designer's experimentation with media and form. In her biography of Greiman, appended to the issue, Friedman writes: "She not only stretched the imagery, but she expands the ideas . . . images that challenge previous conceptions of the limits of graphic vision" (Greiman 1986).

The work remains a personal declaration of independence (Greiman devoted eight pages of *Hybrid Imagery* to its reproduction). A thoughtful publication typically consisting of the expected collection of essays and commentaries, this issue confronted the reader. It is, in almost every way, different. A magazine is delivered in an oddly manufactured envelope rather than the comfortable saddle-stitching. Expecting the traditional, the reader is confronted by the question "Does it make sense?" set in reverse type on a cover that is not a cover. The answer is provided by a second quote from Wittgenstein: "If you give it sense, it makes sense." The audience assumes responsibility for a contribution to a purposefully subjective communication. Evocation of meaning is not difficult when

confronted by this ingenious collection of images: a time line beginning with the creation of the universe, a disembodied brain, dinosaurs, spray cans, a moonscape, spirals, apparently unintelligible scrawls, hands creating geometric figures, the nude portrait, Greiman's second portrait, and fragments of dreams. At the bottom of the front page of the issue, another Wittgenstein aphorism is accompanied by a second head, eyes open, marked as "spiritual double": "In both cases there is a picture in the foreground, but the sense lies in the background."

The single sheet is 25½ inches by 76½ inches, folded into forty-two pages and placed in a slipcase. The reverse contains production notes and color video imagery. Photographs of videoscreen images are incorporated to provide texture. Produced entirely on the Macintosh with MacDraw, the issue was printed out on 8½ inch by 11 inch sheets of bond paper and then brought together for printing. Greiman's original intention was altered both by the computer and by production opportunities: "My idea for the issue was to do it as a 2′ by 6′ poster" (Greiman 1990, 60). During discussions with production staff regarding folds and binding, "the piece evolved and grew . . . I naturally let the piece grow to 33 × 76½ inches" (Greiman 1986, 133). The final size was determined by the economics of printing. During the design phase of the project, text was moved from the front of the poster to the back to accommodate a slightly smaller sheet size.

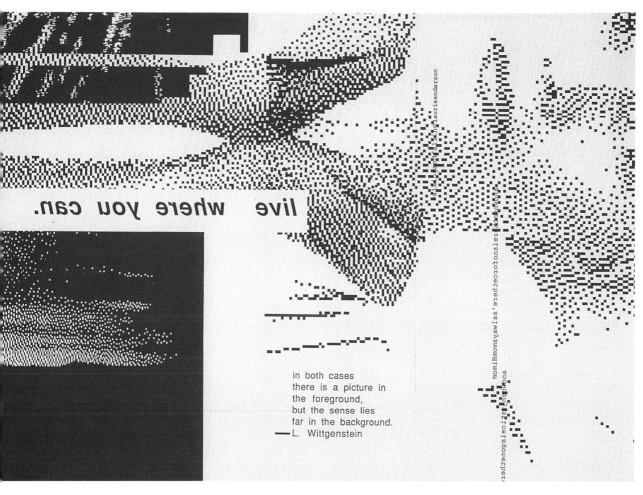

live where you can.

in both cases
there is a picture in
the foreground,
but the sense lies
far in the background.
— L. Wittgenstein

3-4.

April Greiman. *Design Quarterly* 133. Detail. 1986.

Greiman's description of the project is an informative glimpse into her working method and computer design circa 1986: "The genius of MacDraw is that you can input an image/idea and then literally stretch it on screen from a few inches to a few feet in a matter of seconds. . . . You can move things around freely on the surface working at large scale or diving into actual size any time you see fit." "For six months I gathered materials, for three months I sketched (MacPaint) and digitized images (MacVision). For another three months I composed, layered, and stretched (Mac-Draw) and finally produced this piece on the LaserWriter. In the middle of the process it seemed we were perfectly matched—my ideas and ease and speed of my software. It enabled an extraordinary fluidity in a complex creative process. It made possible placing new imagery or text in the space until it became unable to handle all the layering of information I came to want" (Greiman 1986, 133).

The freedom provided by the computer was not freely purchased. The production problems of pioneers are annoying and mysterious.

Ultimately, the speed with which this new technology encouraged me to work throw it into overload. System Errors kept popping up, making it impossible to print out the final image. One night I left the printer on to print overnight, since it takes a fair amount of time to process this much information. In the morning when I returned to the studio I saw the printout had left out the entire bottom half of my body. When I looked at the screen to see what was going on, I noticed that my entire body was no longer there! Everything else layered on top of my former self was plain as day. So, somewhere, near the planet Pluto, we believe, a 5 foot 4$\frac{1}{2}$ inch digitized image of April Greiman is orbiting. (Greiman 1986) Entire days are devoted to trying to figure out how to print the monster. We also learned the hard lesson about making backup copies—a cardinal lesson. (Greiman 1986)

Reflecting later on the process, Greiman concluded that MacDraw was a "friendly, flexible assistant" which, when overcome by its burden, would become "without warning, wildly irrational" (Greiman 1990, 67).

The poster/magazine/issue/manifesto was signed as "made in space by April Greiman." The publication galvanized attention and created dialogues concerning the future roles of the signified and the sign and of digitized communication. With *Does it make sense?* graphic designers were confronted by a technology and a radically different way to order messages within that technology. The image is obviously computerized. It is in no sense primitive.

Maintaining a steady lead ahead of copyists who pursue her style, Greiman's fusion of technology and graphic design has continued to develop. Committed to broadening the limits of communication, her influence on contemporary graphic design has

3-5.

April Greiman. Poster for Museum of Modern Art exhibition, "The Modern Poster," 1988. Video images were laser-scanned and joined in perspective with the Video Paintbox. Generic icons were created using the Macintosh. Video was scanned into the Quantel Graphic Paintbox and manipulated into position. At various stages, traditional and electronic production techniques were integrated. Computer typography and photographically reduced icons were pasted up by hand. The final color comp shown to the client required traditional retouching and airbrushing; these changes were incorporated into the final art electronically.

Design/April Greiman Inc.
Workspace™
87
September 1-2
5th Annual
Moscone Center
San Francisco
Exhibition + Conference for the Office Environment
OPPORTUNITY
CONFLICT
SURVIVAL
SURVIVAL

been prophetic. Refusing to be typecast, she has accepted the primitive "computer look" as a stylistic mannerism and, in other cases, has used the machine to achieve both technically visible and invisible results. A 1988 poster for the Museum of Modern Art shows the influence of computer-generated art within the tradition of the poster. A visual argument for her idea that the "t.v. is the new poster," the design combines the conventional with the computerized.

> I used a television screen as an icon and generated the central image, which was a gradation, by using Image Studio, a good Macintosh retouching program. Then I laser-scanned that into the graphic paint box at super-fine resolution. . . . I can select an area and change its color. I can go out not only to film but to videotape or to printing plates. (Heller 1989, 125)

3-6.

April Greiman. Workspace Poster, 1983. The drop shadows, screen effects, radical geometry, diagonal typography, and essential mystery became a cliche by the mid-1980s. While copyists stole her style, Greiman developed a more sophisticated approach. The client is Western Merchandise Mart (opposite).

Compared with earlier work still influenced by New Wave explosiveness, the poster is sophisticated yet no less enigmatic in its signification. The earlier work is a concentrated effort to produce a stylistic result; the later work is an experiment in the semiotics of technology.

Most recently, Greiman has continued to develop the layering strategy. A billboard created for the 1989 exhibition, Graphic Design in America, for the Walker Art Center is a horizontal, textural timeline. The composite American flag is a blending of the sharp line and stipple of steel engraving, the colored dots of offset lithography, the raster of video, and a mosaic of pixels. Less difficult

3-7.

(above, and next page) April Greiman. Design for Walker Art Center Exhibition, Graphic Design in America, 1989. The billboard/poster was created as a Graphic Paintbox collage. Images were scanned with a digital laser-scanner onto nine-track computer tape, then converted to disk. Layering and blending was performed with Paintbox tools. Final color check and manipulation was completed on the Hell prepress computer system. Output was made onto 4 inch by 5 inch color transparency. Conventional color separations were then created to print posters. The billboard was output on disk as a giant computerized enlargement.

than other projects, and therefore perhaps less interesting to the cognoscenti, the billboard is typical of Greiman's ability to add meaning to a design *by design.* Through her meta-participation as computer graphic designer, the historic reality of change becomes part of the exhibition.

The billboard is exemplary of Greiman's recent mainstreaming within the popular culture not only of California but of the United States. Her March 1990 illustrations for the cover and an interior spread in *Sports Illustrated* embrace a more ecumenical audience. Comparatively reserved in style because of the national and conservative character of the client, the illustrations nevertheless spread the message of technology to a greater whole.

Two recent projects emphasize the intrinsically human character of graphic design. Posters for the Southern California Institute of Architecture and UCLA, each created in 1991, feature the human hand as a dominant thematic image. Found in the CalArts and Spacemat projects of 1978, *Does it make sense?* in 1986, the Workspace poster of 1987, and throughout the design of *Hybrid Imagery: the fusion of technology and graphic design* (1990), the hand is emblematic of Greiman's essentially personal intent: to communicate.

Having mastered the computer, both Greiman and the medium are manifest. An assumption of contradiction between technology and the individual has been shattered. "I continue to stress experiment, the

3-8.

April Greiman. Summer Programs Poster, 1991. The 50 inch by 60 inch design was created for the Southern California Institute of Architecture.

3-9.

April Greiman. University of California, Los Angeles (UCLA) Poster. The human touch is apparent in this image created in the summer of 1991. The photographed hand, an elegant turnabout on the fingerprint motif of contemporary design, has been a motif in Greiman's work since the 1970s (see next page).

exploration of new tools, and the expression of a personal agenda as our reason for being" (Greiman 1990, 156). Computer graphic design need not be impersonal. This way may be as essentially human as the creation of calligraphy with a reed. Each stroke is determined by the artist; each touch of the brush to paper is visible. So with the computer.

Computer graphic design can be both visible and human. Designers have feared the control of the medium. There remains consternation that the computer forces work to "look" a certain way—detached, impersonal, "technological." A consideration of our recent visual history belies this notion. There is no aesthetic or individual risk. Greiman, the most visible exploiter of the medium, is also the most personal of graphic designers.

A different and unique reaction to technology has occurred in Japan. Whether owing to a greater sophistication, a more highly developed cultural appreciation for refined design, or an earlier awareness of capabilities, several Japanese designers did not require the same learning curve as others throughout the world. The anger of primitivism never achieved prominence. By 1985, this design culture was already responsible for relentlessly impressive graphics of postmodern proportion. Several designers were regularly producing work unlike that being done elsewhere. Mitsuo Katsui contends that "Originality in art is closely related to the technology of design" (Thornton 1991, 224). This could be true in very few places. Fortunately, the visibly Japanese construction of a national computer design style does not seem to be globally replicable. No one seems to have done, or is doing, work explicitly like the Japanese (except, of course, the Japanese). The intrinsic value of this work for the rest of the world has been a technological, rather than stylistic, example. As Japanese designers first discovered and mastered the computer, and then transformed the machine's yield into their benefit, other designers understood that they could do the same. Although not copied, the style is influential.

Mitsuo Katsui's *Zero* is a later example. The abstract character of the poster characterizes those designers who have moved directly from a Bauhaus influence to high tech without a significant intervening Pop period. An emphasis on sophisticated design and printing technology is joined by an educated enchantment with rhythmic line and geometric form.

Japanese graphic design is certainly not monolithic, a fact made quite clear in Richard Thornton's extraordinary history, *The Graphic Spirit of Japan* (1991). Nevertheless, graphic designers as stylistically contradictory as Tadanori Yokoo and Ikko Tanaka have been influenced by the purity and simplicity of repeated line. A strong and consistent feature of Japanese design since at least the 1950s, these effects had seminal effect in the development of a prototypically technological alliance that is uniquely Japanese. The most visible of these designers, each remarkably individualistic in style, are Kazumasa Nagai and Takenobu Igarashi.

Nagai creates an ultramodern universe of rainbow starbursts, computerized airbrush effects, repeated line, mesmerizing grids, and mechanical textures. His trademark effect, the deep perspectival line, was developed early on in his career. He communicates concisely and geometrically, joining with designers such as Katsui and Yusaku Kamekura in a celebration of spiked lines and abstract color relationships. Born in 1929 and educated as a sculptor at the Tokyo University of Fine Arts and Music, he developed his design skills throughout the 1950s. When the Nippon Design Center (now the largest design group in the world) was formed in 1959, Nagai was one of its youngest art directors and was

3-10.

Kazumasa Nagai. Logotype
of Nippon Design Center.
The Center has used this
symbol since 1960.

3-11.

Kazumasa Nagai. Poster,
Kawakichi Co., Ltd. 1974.

commissioned to create the group's logotype. He served as president of the Design Center until 1987.

The consistently abstract ground of Nagai's work is, at times, joined by cultural icons. While clouds, sumo wrestlers, geisha, the sea, mountains, flowers, and kanji characters populate posters which are meticulously rendered, the futuristic effect has been consistent. Before and after the computer, Nagai's personal vocabulary emphasized the technical. In a 1974 poster for Kawakichi Co., Ltd., a set of three circular grids float over a surrealist universe of inverted order. The sunset is below the mountains; the sky hovers above.

In a 1982 poster, the same juxtaposition is visible. Whether the sky is above or the sea below, the technical is joined by, and perhaps imposes on, natural order. The comment is in keeping with Nagai's belief that the graphic designer must express not only for himself but to and for a social order. Though the means used to describe his concerns may be clouded in abstraction, Nagai believes that a growing economy may endanger the Japanese culture and environment. His frequent use of traditional icons and natural elements is a reminder of his individual sensibility to societal problems.

Nagai's most famous image celebrates the centenary of Toyama Prefecture. His dependence on nature as theme is only apparently abandoned. A full spectrum of color represents the joy of celebration. The chromatic mountain is formed by rays of

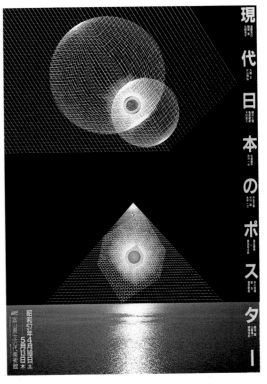

3-12.
Kazumasa Nagai. Poster for the Exhibition, "Contemporary Japanese Posters," Museum of Modern Art, Toyama. The use of cube, sphere, and pyramid is a comment both on the nature of Japanese poster design and Nagai's own work. He does not believe his exhibition posters should presage the work within. In *The Annual of Advertising Art in Japan 85—86*, he concludes that "instead of laying emphasis on one big work from among the many on exhibit, I try to express the event itself. I believe that posters are independent . . . they play the role of visual prelude to an exhibition."

3-13.
Kazumasa Nagai. Poster for the Exhibition, "Kazumasa Nagai Quebec." The touring exhibition was sponsored by the Gallery Nurihiko. 1982.

永井一正カナダ巡回展

3-14.

Kazumasa Nagai. Poster for the exhibition, "100 Paintings of Toyama by 100 Artists," held in conjunction with the centennial celebration of the Prefecture. The three typographic lines set vertically in center identify the centennial and period of the exhibition. At the left are the names of the Museum of Modern Art, Toyama, and the sponsor, Kawakichi Co., Ltd. 1983. Museum of Modern Art, Toyama.

3-15.

Kazumasa Nagai. Poster for the Exhibition, "Tradition et Nouvelles Techniques, 12 Graphistes Japonais." The exhibition was sponsored by Toppan Printing Co., Ltd., and the French Ministry of Culture. 1984.

color flowing from three geometric shapes colored in primaries and perspectivally located between the mountain and the stylized waves of the Japan Sea in the foreground. Nagai is predicting a possible future for Toyama: the vitality of both mountain and sea combine to form beauty and color. "Toyama Prefecture faces the Japan Sea, and there's a mountain range of Tate-yama, which is called the Japan Alps, behind. I tried to visualize the energy of Toyama Prefecture for its future together with the Japan Sea and the mountain range of Tate-Yama" (Gottschall 1989, 197).

The poster is an excellent example of Nagai's use of purposeful technology. The image itself is definitively Japanese. Technology makes possible a masterful visual statement about color and about the world. Repetitive line patterns are easily ordered by using the computer, as are color specifications. A second poster celebrating the 1983 centennial emphasizes typography and the golden setting suns. The names of the painters exhibited in "100 Paintings of Toyama by 100 Artists" are set horizontally. Pyramids of repeated line create a technical Tateyama in the foreground.

In the mid-1980s, Nagai explored the capabilities of the computer. The marriage to an existing style has resulted in an explosively productive oeuvre that has been criticized as repetitive. Nagai's response has been to continue to develop his style within the constraints of his belief that a poster design need not be "about" the event or exhibition it

heralds. His prolific use of the perspectival line and vibrant color has been encouraged by the computer's power to repeat itself.

The relationship between color value and technology is best represented by the work itself. A superior color range, rapid availability of technology, and impeccable printing quality have favored Japanese computer graphic designers. Nagai is among those who have benefited. His work was internationally recognized by the mid-1980s. The 1984 exhibition, "Tradition et Nouvelles Techniques, 12 Graphistes Japonais" represented a foray into France which, by this time, was not unusual. A more disparate collection of colors is used. The playfulness of a 1980s aesthetic is more evident.

In Nagai's recent work, the influence of both technology generally and the computer specifically has, if possible, become more visible. The 1987 poster for the "4-G.D. Posters and Marks" exhibition, though mindful of Nagai's love of traditional natural forms, repeats and extends the style. The spiked lines, the cultural icon, the photograph of clouds, and the geometric shapes have been noticed earlier. Here, however, the burst of lines at the top of the image are more energetic, less controlled, than before. New technology appears to have provided a greater access to free expression.

Explorations continued in posters for the 1989 World Design Expo and the 1988 Store Automation Show. Though the design for the 1989 World Design Expo is more solidly related to earlier work, and therefore

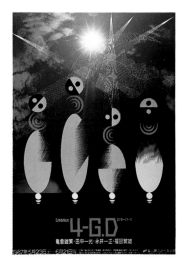

3-16.

Kazumasa Nagai. Poster for the Exhibition, "4-G.D. Posters and Marks" at the Museum of Modern Art, Toyama. The geometric figures are stylistically related to American Postmodernists educated in the Cranbook strategy of layering technological motifs. 1987.

3-17.

Kazumasa Nagai. Poster for the 1988 Store Automation Show. Created for Nippon Keizai Shinbun (Economic Newspaper Co.), there is a noticeable reference to the Bauhaus sensibility. Pure line creates three infinite perspectives. Contemporary design and culture has sufficiently influenced Nagai's style so that intent is understandable only within the postmodernist context.

世界デザイン博覧会

昭和64年7月—11月

財団法人世界デザイン博覧会協会

WORLD DESIGN EXPOSITION '89   DESIGN EXPO '89   NAGOYA, JAPAN, 1989 JUL.-NOV

3-18.

Kazumasa Nagai. Poster
for World Design
Exposition, 1989, Nagoya.
A more obvious reference
to Nagai's own
development as a graphic
designer. The forms are
comparable to his 1974
poster for Kawakichi Ltd.

requires less creative risk, each poster contributes to a recognizable development. As
the designer is freed to create, energy need
not be expended in inking each and every
line. The decision process becomes more
profound; the depth of abstraction is deeper.
It becomes clearer, as for example in the
1988 poster, that a determination is being
made to locate each line specifically where
the designer believes it should be placed.
Nothing is random. Provided new levels of
control, the designer may refine a personal
mode of expression. Developing throughout
his career, and building on his own manner,
Nagai has generated a uniquely technological
form of abstract expressionism.

The graphic expressionism of Takenobu Igarashi is different in both form and intent from that of either April Greiman or Kazumasa Nagai. Using technology to create a very new forum for design, Igarashi has developed the form, manner, technique, and medium of *space graphics,* a position that is neither Japanese nor non-Japanese. It is, simply, his own.

As with Greiman and Nagai, Igarashi does not permit technology to dominate approach. Educated at Tama University and the University of California at Los Angeles, his work is structured by his appreciation for sculpture and the human condition. After opening his office in 1970, he began experimentations with manipulations of letterforms in two and three dimensions. Before he adopted the computer in order to fully develop this unique and new technological form, Igarashi had begun to generate symbols based on new "space-age" laws of perspective.

A 1983 sculpture series, *AL 070783,* represents one of Igarashi's first encounters with the possibilities provided by the computer. Demonstrating his visual philosophy, "design for design," the series consists of three-dimensional letters of the Roman alphabet manufactured according to Igarashi's guidelines. Exhibited at the Mikimoto Hall in Toyko and then at the Reinhold Brown Gallery in New York, "each of the sculptures is made up of a number of thick and thin aluminum plates joined together by screws. For the first time I used a computer-controlled laser to cut the plates. A metal brush was used on the surface to give it more texture" (Gottschall 1989, 199). The letters are each about 5½ inches tall. Other Igarashi multidimensional letters are much larger. His directory signage for the Toranomon NN Building in Tokyo, for example, consists of four adjoining uppercase Ns forming a square twelve feet high. The impressions caused by these monumental letters offer insight into his purpose. They are not his most famous medium.

Isometric art may involve the complete abandonment of perspective. The elegance of this discovery, aided by the computer, provided Igarashi with a unique way to escape the flatness of the page. Rather than "layer in" to avoid the bleakness of intellectual and visual monotony—rather than copy another designer's solution—Igarashi invented his own way.

Space graphics are isometric shapes in which three dimensions are shown not in perspective but in their "actual" measurements. The sculptural shapes can be manipulated in an infinite number of ways. In practice, the result are letters or characters that reach the heights of architectural form. Each design element is drawn to identical height and width. Igarashi intends to create what he calls a "visual transformation." He believes this change in an individual viewer's relationship to the world of design is necessary for both the viewer and for graphic design. Believing that graphic design is a harmonizing force within society, Igarashi has

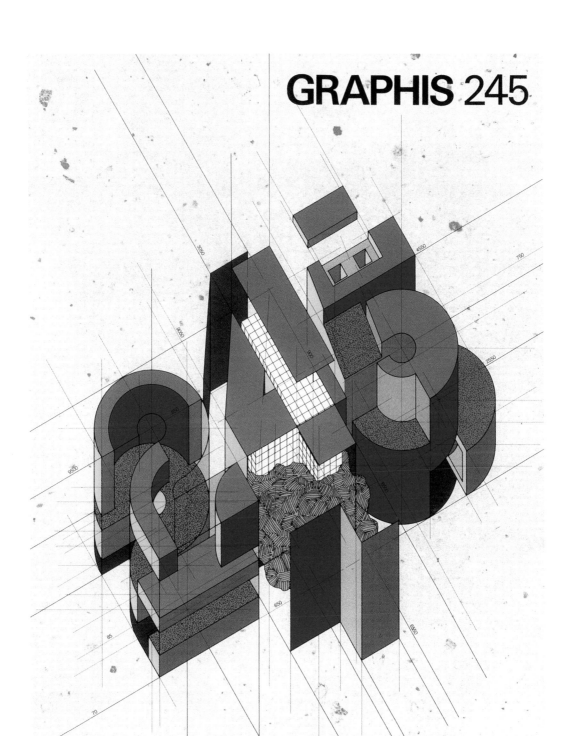

GRAPHIS 245

3-19.

Takenobu Igarashi. Isometric illustration
for the cover of *Graphis* 245. September/
October 1986. Igarashi has used the
isometric form for posters, corporate
clients, information graphics,
and (perhaps most appropriately in a
visual sense) three-dimensional objects.

sought ways to make the products of his profession more integrally related to real lives.

Space graphics is an attempt to humanize the postmodern environment. These structures are extremely complicated, yet inviting. Geometric shapes form playful invitations of color and texture. For one project, a calendar for the Museum of Modern Art in New York, Igarashi created over six hundred figures. The 1985 calendar featured different isometric numerals each day. A more widely recognized project for the museum was his design for a shopping bag. The collection of white dots on black forms several geometric shapes and patterns. As with Igarashi's isometric shapes, the viewer is invited to participate in the design, to ask questions, and to formulate answers. The corporate coolness of monochrome dots does not countermand Igarashi's insistence that a dialogue must be engaged.

As might be expected of a designer so concerned with his fellow inhabitants of the planet, Igarashi joins the most productive computer graphic designers in his refusal to rely on the computer. As in the past, his most recent works are the result of the combined efforts of hand and machine. He does not believe the computer can provide ideas. Rather, he brings that vision to the computer when he believes the tool best serves the process.

The Macintosh has not contributed to any changes in our design approach. For a long time, we were practicing methods and ways of thinking that are characterized by a computer,

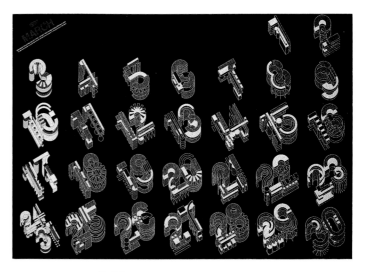

3-20.

Takenobu Igarashi. The month of March 1991, from the Alphabet Gallery. The Gallery produces annual poster calendars created by Igarashi. This example is typical of Igarashi's use of graphics to create illusory three-dimensional space. In this particular project, the letterforms were created by hand.

3-21.

Takenobu Igarashi. The month of March 1989, commissioned by Zanders Feinpaipere AG. Produced with the Mac Plus in 1987 and 1988. The computer is used with alacrity and without visual effect. It is impossible to distinguish Igarashi's computerized work from graphics created entirely by hand. The studio continues to use both hand and computerized methods, at times combining the two forms in the same project (opposite, top).

3-22.

Takenobu Igarashi. Shopping bag, Museum of Modern Art, New York, 1985 (opposite, bottom).

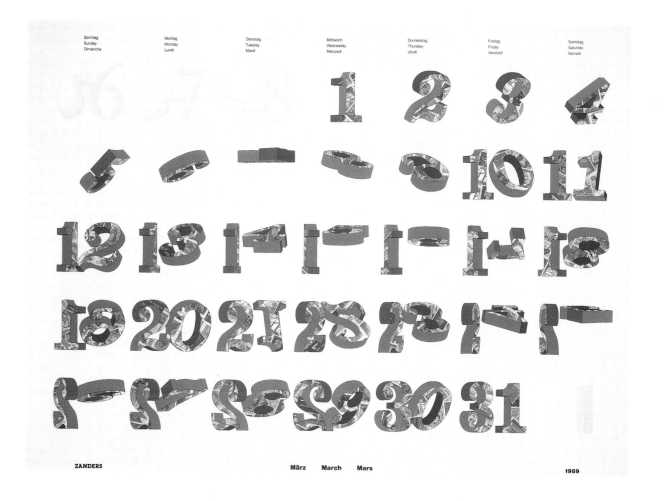

3-23.

Takenobu Igarashi. Poster, Kanagawa Prefecture Art Festival, 1984. Although Igarashi had used the computer for several projects by this time, this poster and the 1985 MOMA shopping bag are technical expositions produced without the use of technology. Created entirely by hand (next page).

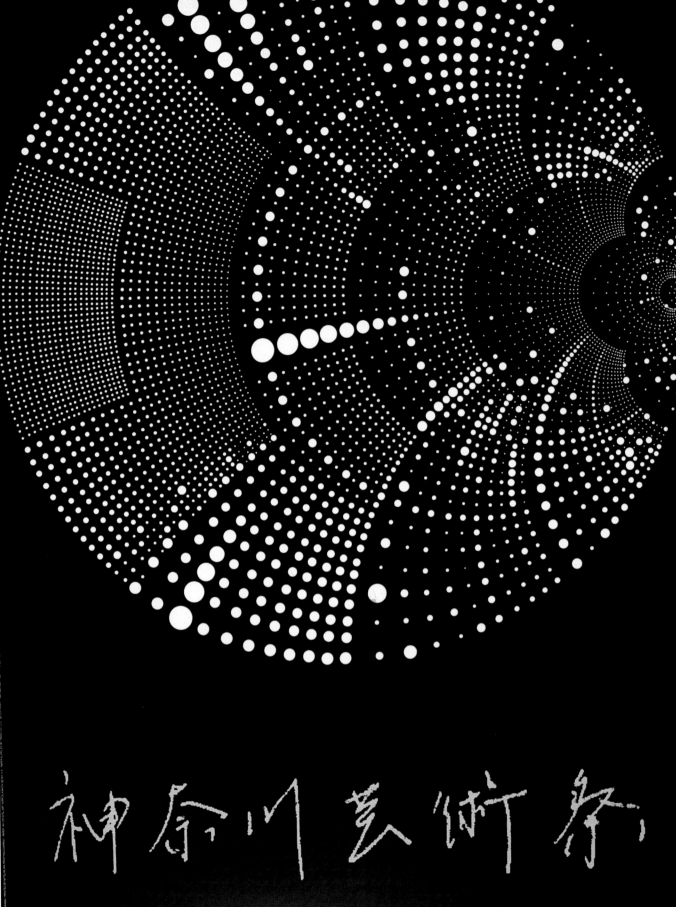

神奈川芸術祭

第9回(昭和59年度)神奈川芸術祭／昭和59年10月〜12月／音楽　演劇 舞踊 古典芸能 美術 映画・放送 文芸／主催:神奈川県

before using the computer itself . . . working on a computer enables us to do what is impossible by hand. Also, we can let the computer perform difficult or troublesome chores. (*Emigre II, 3*)

By invoking and visually insisting upon our participation, Igarashi believes he is improving the quality of individual existence. This humanistic agenda has as its immediate goal the establishment of paths of communication between and among the computer graphic designer and the viewers of work. His success in meeting that objective may be accurately measured by the international appreciation of his work. Although not influential in the same sense as April Greiman, Igarashi's work is no less significant as a statement of the contemporary condition.

AFTERWORD

The primitive computer graphic designer may believe that a joint communicative effort between designer and viewer is no longer probable. Semiotics tells us that there can be no interpretation without the interconnection of signs. If we miss connections, we do not discover the parts of the message that create structure. We make new connections to replace those we have missed. Communication, and perhaps meaning as well, is lost. In a world in which primitives believe all meaning is relativistic, legibility is perceived to be an anachronism. Typeface design can be radically changed.

There is a powerful, seemingly elemental, push toward anomie, toward the other, toward the stranger, in contemporary aesthetics. Once recognized, British Punk accepted this urge and condemned graphic design to nihilism. The designers discussed in this chapter are equally aware of this push; they have, however, individually accepted a challenge and responsibility. Working within an environment that some believe is value-free and valueless, they share the common belief that computer graphic design is a means to achieve meaning in the universe of contemporary media.

The message of these designers is not transparent or easy to understand. Communication requires an intelligent act of interpretation. These designers insist that the individual is an essential contributor to the design process. The viewer is involved in the essential, humanizing act of understanding.

Participation becomes the thoughtful designer's answer to anonymity. The computer brain, that monster of the 1950s sci-fi movie which still lurks in our cultural subconscious, is turned back on itself. A new tool is used to salvage the integrally human act of understanding. But without the ideas and work of these designers, the machine contributes nothing. We must acknowledge the computer graphic designer, and not the computer, as the essential ingredient in this effort.

4

HIDDEN MACHINES

Computers are us. The profits to be gained through software and hardware are conspicuously consumed. The need to know about computers is no longer discussed. The term "computer literacy" announces the prominence and scope, achieved in nanosecond time, of a new technology within our culture. Growth in our language does not occur randomly. The new vocabulary carries with it new meaning.

A decade ago, before the introduction of the IBM PC, we understood the computer only as the source of fabled errors and the legend, "Do not fold, spindle, or mutilate" on a Hollerith punch card that no longer exists. Few knew what a bit or a disk drive was. No one could have identified a mouse. Now, we have begun to assume that the ability to use a computer is as vital a life-skill as reading. One of the self-defining questions of an earlier decade was "When did you come out against the war?" The contemporary replacement is "When did you buy your first PC?" Happy are those who can claim to have bought a Heath Kit in 1976.

The joy of techno-victory soon fades. Technology develops so rapidly that the computer literati have no time to savor their success. No sooner is one trail blazed than another awaits. A more cautious group moves in to discover what good can actually be done on the ground provided. The contribution of the next wave of exploration is less visible and unconditionally required.

Invisibility offers advantages. Graphic designers who abandon the T-square and exacto knife without notice are not compelled to sacrifice a hard-won approach to subject matter. The computer may be kept aesthetically closeted without prejudice to the user. Design professionals may legitimately decide to use the technology as a tool. The work of those who have developed critically meaningful (and visible) computer design styles does not diminish the work of those who choose not to do so.

Technical control, increased speed, and cheaper costs are mundane reasons to use technology. They are unquestionably popular. There are, however, prices and prerequisites. John Sherman of the University of Notre Dame points out that "Designers today face a new requirement: to acquire & master a digital craft" (Sherman 1991, 191). Mastering technology demands a high level of skill and a dedication to learning. The casual user never fully understands the symphony of commands required of and by the professional. Irrespective of advertising claims

offering quick solutions and easy answers, computer graphic design is an achievement. Software is not often serendipitous. An investment must be made in an educational process that is not much less frustrating than learning how to draw lines with a technical pen. The demands of this craftsmanship are different but no less rigorous.

Graphic designers who do master the digital skills realize unforeseen gains. Beyond the advantages of technical ability and economics, the computer permits the graphic designer to quickly visualize possibilities. The process is not faster or easier—the computer brain still lags far behind the human brain in any creativity race. Many computer graphic designers (including John Hersey, Nancy Skolos, and April Greiman) continue to sketch with pencil. Once at the screen, however, the process of creating comprehensives is more spontaneous. Design elements can be distorted, enlarged, reduced, or eliminated. Graphics can be manipulated in and out of position quickly. Chromatic choices are readily available. For many, these creative advantages are the fundamental reason to spend the days and hours necessary to become digital masters. But the computer does not anticipate aesthetic choices.

These computer graphic designers have made the decision to use technology in a certain way. The motivation varies with the individual. The instrument has been sufficiently developed to accommodate a wider range of choice. No longer must rasters and pixels be visible. The medium is opaque. The creator has the power to make decisions. Soon, computer graphic design will become, quite simply, graphic design. Every graphic designer will be a computer graphic designer. Already, as we so rapidly matured, there are those who have developed or refined an individual manner without stylistic reliance on the medium. Their work is as much a harbinger of a possible design future as the most radically pixelated statement.

Perhaps ironically, the work of Apple Creative Services has never looked like it has been designed with a computer. Everything is. Though its identity position has frequently changed since Apple's formation in 1977, Creative Services has consistently used the computer to create the required public image. As founders of an unknown computer start-up, Steven Jobs and Steve Wozniak understood the gravity of corporate graphic design. The first graphics of the company featured a four-color identity mark. While IBM's logo was big and blue, Apple's was small and brash, and was green, yellow, red, and blue (and, at times, as many other colors of the rainbow as possible). One of the first small firms to capitalize on the suggestion that a corporation could actually be its corporate identity, Apple created itself in its own image. In time, identity became reality. As creative director Michael Markman put it, Apple succeeded in its hope to "become everything that it pretended to be" (Pearlman 1989, 38). Graphic design was a substantial contributor to the birth process.

In 1982, Thomas Suiter and Clement Mok were enlisted in the Apple design program. "Before Suiter, it seemed that anything went. Seeing how many colors you could throw at design was the norm" (Aaland 1989, 44). Creative directors Suiter and Mok were joined by Thomas Hughes and illustrator John Casado. Positioned as the innovative alternative to IBM, Apple's antiestablishment image was supported by a carefree, colorful style. Packaging, advertising, and corporate communications carried the same message: computer people didn't have to be intractable sales types wearing uniform dark suits. "The computer for the rest of us" was friendly, easy to use, and relentlessly satisfying. Presenting the product as the intelligent yet unconventional option, Apple's campaign was traditional in both style and intent. Apple as "revolutionary Fortune 500 company" is a contradiction in terms; the success of the company is based on that understanding. The company was designed to be neither big or blue.

Reflecting conventional standards of graphic excellence, computer design messages accompanied an opportune theme. The consequence was an extremely successful campaign, or as Apple advertising puts it, a happy ending. Interesting computer graphics worked. They were not revolutionary. "The challenge was to create the visual identity for a totally new technology standard and translate that identity into all packaging, sales literature, point of purchase displays, instruction manuals, video demo-stations, screen icons, signage, and multi-media presentations" (Mok 1987, 26). As creative director involved in the planning and execution of all promotional materials introducing the Macintosh, Mok defined the power of liberation. A graphic aesthetic aided in creating a cultivated Apple mystique that was not necessarily his own. Experimentally, he has worked in the quite different direction of the primitive. Demonstrating his belief that the communication requirements of the individual client must preside over the development of a

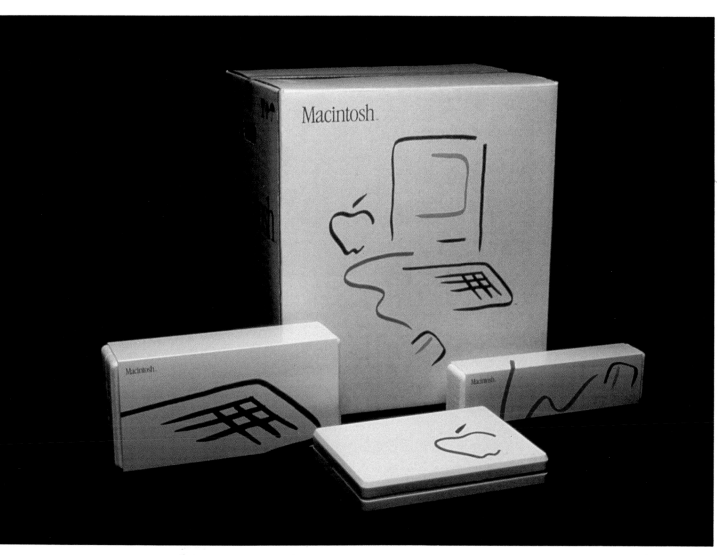

4-1.

Clement Mok. Package designs for the
Apple Macintosh. Freehand drawing and a
multicolored aesthetic were the
fundamental characteristics of a campaign
that positioned Apple as the happy
alternative to monolithic IBM.

transcendent personal style, Mok has been an innovator of a different order. The objective of graphic design is communication. Personal expression is not a necessary aspiration. It may be a disservice.

The potential for conflict between the aesthetic and the communicative functions of graphic design is continuous. The problem is magnified by the demands of the corporate voice. Mok has been able to carefully combine an interest in computer graphic design with an abiding ability to independently develop within the constraints of his profession. Two recent logotypes are exemplary. Mok uses a nontraditional technology, the computer, to provide interesting yet suitably conservative solutions.

Visual puns are part of a California convention Mok has done much to construct. The use of the cartoon as an illustration approach is also typical of a lighter approach. Whether isometric or unidimensionally stylized, the computerized cartoon accomplishes specific goals. Different messages are sent by different clients. A recent package design, produced in the Retro mannerism influenced by rediscovered Art Deco, reflects yet another aesthetic. The lesson learned is that style can be intelligently and courageously subservient to the demands of communication.

Apple Creative Services has consistently demonstrated that philosophy in its tremendous output over a period of fifteen years. Producing up to 3500 projects annually, with a printing budget in the tens of millions of dollars, Creative Services is

4-2.

Clement Mok. Exhibit design for Macintosh. The rainbow Apple symbol and carefree meander reinforce the Apple market position.

4-3.

Clement Mok. Experimental graphic reproduced in *Pacific Wave*, quite unlike the clean designs offered to corporate clients. The two-page spread is headed by a quotation from Antonio Machado: "To see things as they are, the eyes must be open; to see things as other than they are, they must be open even wider; to see things as better than they are, they must be open to the full." Two hands holding the design elements emerge from clouds in foreground. Graphics are reproduced on verso and recto to intimate a human face. 1987.

4-4.
Clement Mok. Logotype,
Connect. The simple use
of a hyphen offers no
indication of a computer
aesthetic.

4-5.
Clement Mok. Logotype,
Pillar. The visual pun is
facilitated by the
dangerous ease with
which letterforms may be
altered by professional
and amateur alike. Here
Mok makes good use of
the capability.

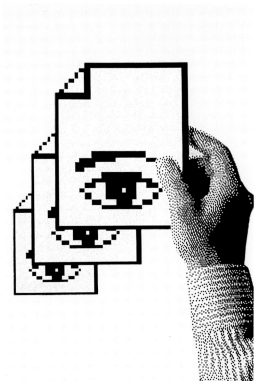

4-6.
Clement Mok. The colorful implications of computerized dot patterns and stylized human figure reflects the easygoing manner of American Punk (see previous page).

4-7.
Clement Mok. Package design for Macromind Director. The influence of Retro concretized by manipulation of advanced technology. In the 1980s and 1990s, Retro designers have created a design style based on the principle of eclectic borrowing from the past.

responsible for the articulation of in-house communication design. Clarity and the computer have been the two consistent factors to survive several generations of design intent. With ninety graphic designers, art directors, illustrators, and video artists on staff, the maintenance of corporate consistency is the responsibility of creative director Tim Brennan. In 1985, the image shifted from friendly alternative to Serious Contender. Creative director Paul Pruneau forged a tough campaign that challenged IBM's market position. The Apple symbol was made more precise; an elegant old style roman typeface, Garamond, was chosen as the vehicle of Apple language.

Several years later, Apple found its way back to its affable roots. The stylistic pendulum convinced Brennan to produce a supplement to the corporate identity manual. The poster is typical of the manner in which Apple designers carefully incorporate the Apple manner into in-house graphics. The typographic format, appearance, and demand for quality is equivalent to that of Apple advertising.

Creative Services is not exclusively concerned with print media. The budget for printing the Apple message onto fabrics is said to be in the millions of dollars. Organized according to "skill clusters" that have included corporate graphics, education, computer graphics, art direction, trade shows and events, packaging/3-D, and video, Apple's in-house design staff is among the largest such facility in the world. Many are actively involved in research and develop-

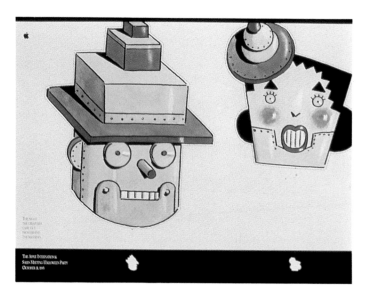

4-8.
Clement Mok. Isometric cartoon figures for an Apple special event.

4-9.
Mark Drury, Carl Stone, and Richard Binell. Poster for Apple Computer exhibition, International Design Aspen. The use of Garamond is typical; the alteration of the Apple symbol is not. 1988.

No.

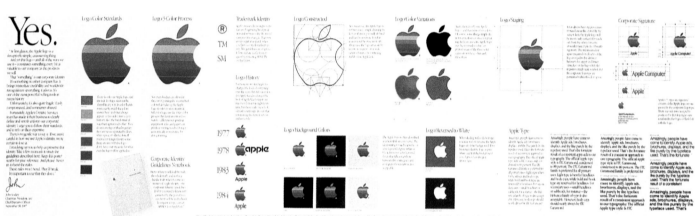

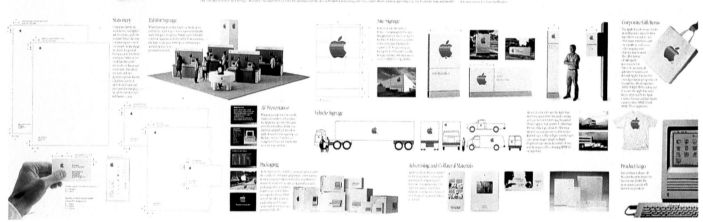

4-10.

Tim Brennan and Rob Gemmell, art
directors. Jill Savini, designer. Poster
design, Apple Computer. This supplement
to Apple's corporate identity manual
displays the proper and improper use of
the Apple symbol.

ment. "The technology has become so complex . . . we live it on a daily basis" (Aaland 1989, 44). Hugh Dubberly, an Apple creative director who has also served as chairman of the computer graphics department at Art Center College of Design, has fostered Apple's interest in interactive computer applications. One of the first to experiment with hypermedia, Dubberly ensures that Apple staff use the software the corporation hopes to sell.

Disagreeing with those who would keep the computer completely invisible, Dubberly contends that the computer is not just another tool. Agreeing with Greiman and Nagai, he believes that new software has created potential futures we must decide to design. "Computers are not just fancy typewriters. Computers are not just new ways of doing the same old things. Computers are also a way of doing new things—unexpected things. Here is the promise of technology. . . . It is magic—the magic dream of a better world" (Dubberly 1991, 37). Dubberly and Doris Mitsch have developed new hypermedia applications, including interactive sales literature and scientific learning tools.

As early as 1987, the Apple annual report and other significant projects were being completed with hypermedia. "We went from seeing the Mac as a tool used only for another medium (print) to actually being a

medium in its own right" (Pearlman 1989, 41). A teaching tool, the Knowledge Navigator, attracted national attention in 1988. Developed by Apple Fellow James Kay and Nicholas Negroponte, director of the MIT Media Laboratory, the software was a first glimpse at a program that looked like a computer book, recognized the spoken word, combined words and pictures to answer individualized questions, and delivered information from an electronic library. The essence of the interactive process cannot be captured on this printed page.

Dubberly and other experimenters at Creative Services have offered visions of possible futures. The potential is a marvelous unknown: "We have a chance to do things never done before. We have a chance to explore, to invent the future. It's time to get started" (Dubberly 1991, 41). Stressing the importance of graphic design education in developing truly literate computer designers, he has helped to organize forward motion. That service would be sufficient to earn praise for any corporation. To that contribution is added the value of Clement Mok and Apple Creative Services, and the significance of Macintosh in the development of the computer as design tool. The image created by Jobs and Wizniak in 1977 has been realized. Apple impact on computer graphic design has been nothing less than prophetic.

By 1983, Lance Hidy had developed a graphic message meriting a book-length exposition. Having spent years creating a means to achieve his goals, it is not unexpected that he did not radically alter his style on discovering the computer. After the development of sufficiently sophisticated paint and color graphic software, the computer was accepted as pragmatically valuable.

Best known as an illustrator, Hidy was educated at Yale University. After graduation, he worked for over ten years as a typographer, book designer, and illustrator, most notably with David R. Godine. He opened his own studio in 1974, and within several years began to concentrate on the poster art which has become his most important contribution to contemporary graphics. His first two posters, created for the Beardsley's Cafe Restaurant in 1977 and 1978, are early examples of his ability to use color to achieve and evoke emotion. In the 1980s, his work was influential in the development of Color-Field Design, a pattern built on the foundation of Hokusai, Beatrix Potter, the Beggarstaffs, cartoon art, the Push Pin Studio, Ivan Chermayeff, and David Lance Goines. Flat color, organic shape, expressiveness, and simplicity are its hallmarks. Color becomes image and emotional message. Facilitating an increased ability to control shape and make surgical adjustments in chromatic value, the computer was rapidly accepted by many color-field designers.

Hidy exploits the quiet feeling evoked by simple color planes. Building on a stylistic elegance owing much to his work in the private press tradition, Hidy captures the essence of his subject through abstraction. He takes great care to accurately demarcate geographic lines. Though the fields are never haphazard and often geometric, chromatic values insist on the creation of inviting, organic form. Conspicuously opposed to the notion that the medium should be apparent in the work, Hidy believes with Beatrice Warde and the crystal goblet school of the 1930s that "the hand of the designer must be subordinated to the transmission of the message" (Fern 1983, 45).

As Hidy develops a mature style, the ability to connect with a viewer is augmented by specific additions to the vocabulary. The best work involves the viewer immediately. We supply missing elements to the message; abstract elements are mentally transformed into objects from a real world. Participation through closure has become an integral phrase in the vocabulary of color-field design. Recent developments in software may have assisted in fostering the rapidity with which this expression has been copied. Using paint software available as early as 1985, the designer is able to rapidly fill or exchange on-screen fields of color. Rather than painting by hand or cutting and placing colored papers, unlimited number of possible color combinations may be instantaneously manufactured. Experimentation is encouraged by a process that is relatively blameless; little time and no

BEARDSLEY'S
CAFÉ RESTAURANT

HIDY

SECOND ANNIVERSARY CELEBRATION
27 JUNE 1977 NORTHAMPTON MASSACHUSETTS

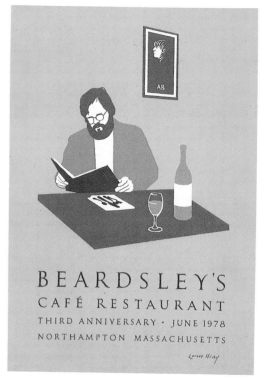

4-11.

Lance Hidy. Poster for Beardsley's Cafe Restaurant, Northampton, Massachusetts. 1977. The hand silkscreen for the poster (25 inches by 16½ inches) was cut by David Stokes. The model is David Barbeau. Background color echoes the welcoming gesture of the waiter. The viewer is harmoniously carried into the scene. Hidy capitalizes on the potential of color to produce subconscious effect.

4-12.

Lance Hidy. Poster for Beardsley's Cafe Restaurant, Northampton, Massachusetts. 1978. Printed by offset lithography, Adams Printing, Templeton, Massachusetts. Size: 25¼ inches by 17½ inches. The model is fellow illustrator Barry Moser. The background color, the color of the patron's coat, and the captured private moment combine to create an instinctive sense of intrusion. Acknowledging the design as an aesthetic failure and an educational success, Hidy accepts the artistic learning process.

4-13.

Lance Hidy. Poster, Davis-Kidd
Booksellers, Memphis, Tennessee. 1990.
Printed by Rob Day of Mink Brook
Editions, West Lebanon, New Hampshire.
Size: 32 inches by 21.5 inches. The absence
of features does nothing to dehumanize
the figures; the viewer interacts with the
illustration to provide the necessary
detail. The communication process is
facilitated.

4-14.

Lance Hidy. Poster, *Stone*. 1989. The model
is type designer Sumner Stone (see Chapter
6). The Stone family is the first to contain
serif, sans serif and informal elements.
Closure informs the picture. We intuit
that the scene exists in a completed
environment. By allowing us to supply these
details, Hidy empowers our participation in
the communication process.

materials are lost as various chromatic decisions are considered and rejected.

In communicating his intent, Hidy is as clear verbally as he is visually. "I have set my artistic goals as clarity, simplicity, durability, and emotion, and the audience I try to reach is the general public" (Fern 1983, 52). When hardware and software proved to be able to support his goals, new technology was reasonably accepted as convenient. The poster most obviously announcing that tacit endorsement was *Stone*, created for Adobe. Although the working process may change, the product has not. Hidy's use of the computer is not visible. The poster reflects the same values expressed in works previously drawn and painted entirely by hand.

In describing his working method before the computer, Hidy notes his reliance on figure drawing skills. His proficiency is apparent; it has required years of course-work and practice. Hidy begins work with the camera. After shooting from 100 to 300 pictures of his subjects in natural positions, Hidy views his slides and selects appropriate images. Drawing from slides provides the opportunity to revise, simplify, shift, and develop images. He refines his drawings as a design takes shape.

The success of the creative process involves several imperatives: an effective style, a working technique, visualization of the image, the appropriate model, photographic abilities, appropriate selection, figure drawing skills, refinement of the image, and painting expertise. These requirements can be provided only by the creative "heart and mind" (Fern 1983, 51). Using canvas or the computer, the human is the only constant. Technology is not sufficient nor even a catalyst. For this illustrator, the invisible computer is at best an accelerator.

It is reasonable to believe that the information design contained in the pages of such publications as *Time, Newsweek,* and *USA Today* has its roots in computer technology. These graphics have the "computer" look: sophisticated, informative, and multilayered images that communicate data verbally and visually. As with Hidy's visual style, however, the form developed independent of computer technology. Although the term became popular in the 1980s, information design has its roots in Cartesian analytical geometry, William Playfair's publication of statistical bar charts and pie charts in the late eighteenth and early nineteenth centuries, and the invention of the science of statistics by Jacques Quetel in the second quarter of the nineteenth century. In the 1920s, Otto Neurath's development of Isotype (International System of Typographic Picture Education) and a "Vienna Method" provided a communications model which was immediately influential. Neurath's influence continues today.

In the 1970s, a new illustrative form developed. Multidimensional graphics became commonplace. The spare repetitions of earlier charts were replaced by layered graphics that communicated more information with added immediacy. Contemporary advances in technology and isometric design spurred the movement toward three dimensions and beyond. The computer was gladly accepted; it provided a means to complete a development that had already begun. In addition, interest was stimulated in new, more sophisticated constructs. The case has been made that "technology dramatically elevated the role and importance of designers" (Morris 1990, 35). As the laser printer fostered new informational demands, both managers and marketers recognized the visual presentation as an essential ingredient in creating the message.

By the mid-1980s, the pages of Gannett's *USA Today,* a new national daily, were splashed with graphics computerized in several senses (including creation, transmittal through telecommunication, and production). High technology was featured in print and broadcast advertising. Information design created by the computer became a marketing tool. When it was made aware of the potential, the public was sold on (and served by) an advanced informational aesthetic. Many information designers, meanwhile, continued to use the traditional metnods of adhesive screen, tapes, amberlith, and pressure-sensitive lettering.

Information designers did not require media attention to glimpse a potential future. By 1984, the technology existed in fact: "the computer is used daily at *The New York Times* and has resulted in a 15- to 20-hour-per-week saving of time taken to produce roughly 74 charts and 48 maps" (Holmes 1984, 65). Gradations of tone and primitive paint effects were already available. Beyond the aesthetics of the machine, however, the two great disadvantages of the mid-1980s

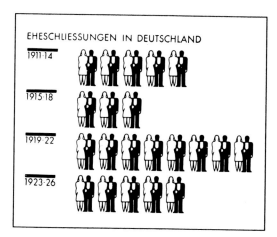

4-15.

Otto Neurath, "Eheschliessungen in Deutschland," Gesellschafts und Wirtschaftsmuseum in Wien (Vienna Museum of Social and Economic Studies), 1927. The chart shows marriage statistics in Germany from 1911 to 1926. The Vienna method emphasized simplicity and the internationalization of communication. Countering the prevalent trend of showing increases in quantity by increasing the size of a symbol, Neurath repeated the symbol as many times as necessary to represent value.

4-16.

Delos Blackmar, "The Banks and Speculation." From Ryllis A. Goslin and Omar P. Goslin, *Rich Man, Poor Man*, a publication of The People's League for Economic Security. Published by Harper & Brothers, New York, 1935. The League's advisory council included John Dewey, Harry Elmer Barnes and Harry A. Overstreet. Futura was used throughout the book. The use of a sans as text type and the acceptance of the Vienna informational method illustrate the impact of the Bauhaus ethos.

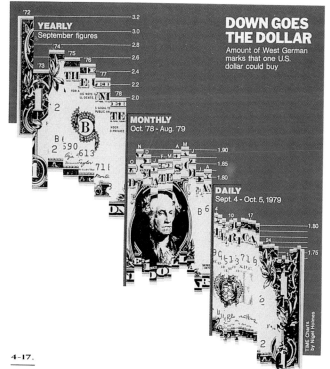

4-17.

Nigel Holmes, "Down Goes the Dollar," reproduced in *Time*. 1979. A chart displaying the dollar's slip against the dollar, 1972 to 1979. Although produced by hand, the graphic is a departure from the serious detachment of earlier models. The resourceful use of the shattered dollar is an example of multidimensional informing not possible through repetition of isotypes.

TELLTALES OF TWO CITIES

Cost of living — New York City — Moscow

	New York City	Moscow
Hours worked per week	39.7	42
Manufacturing worker's earnings per week	$265.60	$56.54
Monthly rental 3-room apt.	$1,000	$37
Heat and electricity per month	$82	$4.50
Bus or subway per ride	50¢	8¢
Car	$6,200 (Citation)	$10,000 (Zhiguli)
Gallon of gasoline	$1.35	$1.25
Vodka (1 liter)	$6	$11
Dental checkup	$32	Free
Ballpoint pen	29¢	$1.50
1 lb. chicken	66¢	$2.55
Pack of cigarettes	75¢	52¢
Loaf of bread (1 lb.)	62¢	24¢
Jeans	$18.50	$45
Man's leather shoes	$42	$45
Vacation (2 weeks per person)*	$910	$120
Woman's dress	$90	$60
Sofa	$600	$260
Gold wedding ring	$75	$225
Hard-cover novel	$12.95	$3
Color television	$710 (25-in. screen)	$1,094 (24-in. screen)
Pantyhose	$1.50	$10
Newspaper	25¢ (Daily News)	5¢ (Izvestiya)
Woman's leather shoes	$33	$40

All figures are typical current prices.

* Vacations: the New York figure represents a peak season cost with meals at a major Florida resort city; 70% of the Moscow figure is paid by the worker's union.

TIME Chart by Nigel Holmes

4-18.
Nigel Holmes, "Telltales of Two Cities," reproduced in *Time*. 1980. The questioning mode of contemporary graphic design. Research reveals a myriad of comparisons between life in Moscow and New York. In New York, a gold wedding ring costs less than two days' pay; in Moscow, it cost nearly five weeks' pay. In New York, rent, electricity and heat combine to cost more than the entire month's salary; in Moscow, a bit over three days' pay. Believing that these figures reveal something, we look for meaning. But we are not told.

were that computing was slow and very expensive. "Their drawback: they cost a million dollars" (Holmes 1984, 65). Discussing a comparatively simple graphic printed for a magazine feature about computers, Nigel Holmes expresses the experimental nature of the period: "This in fact took longer to create than if it had been drawn by hand. But as an exercise in getting a machine to draw exactly what you want, it worked" (Holmes 1984, 69). Information design was aesthetically ready. These disadvantages were eliminated by the late 1980s, unknown to a new generation that could not comprehend how graphics could have been created before the computer. Information design took the lead in exploiting technological advances.

Educated at the Royal College of Art in London, Holmes began work at *Time* in 1978 and later served as Deputy Art Director. Because of the magazine's national and international scope, his graphics were influential (along with *USA Today*) in establishing information design as a popularly understood, distinct category of visual communication. A variety of strategies were used to solve particular problems: flat color, symbols, texture, photography, abstraction, cartoons, and obvious computer imagery. A complicated comparison of life in 1980 New York and Moscow which appeared in *Time* demonstrates the value of information design. The data in this chart could not be understood as quickly or as well in another form. Editorial decisions aside (the Russian side of the table features duller colors, predominant shadows, and less stylish detailing), the graphic features an intriguing use of research. Though not as obviously connected, in visual terms, to the contemporary aesthetic of the shattered dollar, the chart uses a uniquely postmodern stratagem to involve the viewer. Though interested and informed, the reader is involved in a mystery. (For example, in 1980 Moscow, why is vodka more expensive than in New York? Why are cigarettes and books so much cheaper?) The viewer is intrigued by questions not answered.

The work of Richard Saul Wurman and the staff of Access Press, on the other hand, answers questions that have not yet been asked. After studying architecture at the University of Pennsylvania, Wurman worked in Philadelphia as an architect and urban planner until 1976. He later taught at Cambridge University, the University of Southern California, UCLA, and California Polytechnic. In 1981, he founded Access Press. With offices in New York, Access Press and its San Francisco affiliate, The Understanding Business, produce city guides, maps, atlases, and other projects which are visually satisfying and uniquely creative. Wurman has compared information to a series of rooms, some of which are more important than others, some serving others. Recognizing the mediascape, and the informational deluge so dangerous to the process of informing, Wurman uses the computer to facilitate comprehension.

In developing effective means to provide information exchange, he is not so much interested in design as in society. William McCaffrey, head of an advertising agency in New York, notes that Wurman is "dealing with bigger things than most designers encounter in their day-to-day work, things that have an impact on the way people live and think" (Brooks 1990, 122).

The 1985 *Access Guide to Tokyo* tells us about restaurant and museum locations, visa requirements, and transportation schedules. We are also culturally informed. Subway line maps are drawn in the traditional shape of the yin and yang symbol (the actual shape of the subway line is highlighted as a small encircled graphic inside the symbol). Apparently incidental marginalia are in fact a determined attempt to communicate information as painlessly and effectively as possible. Accompanying a map of the Yamanote Line, for example, is a paragraph explaining that over 7 billion passengers use the Japanese National Railways annually. The *San Francisco Access Guide* offers a visual guide to the fare one might expect to find at a dim sum restaurant, advances ordering hints, and explains that only in this city and Hong Kong would one find such a plethora of dim sum. A visitor also discovers a color-coded map of the city's financial district; the colors apprise the reader of the city's rate of development. The cumulative effect of such "fillers" is to provide information that the reader might not otherwise discover. Each representation is determined by Wurman's answer to an essential question, "What is the key to this particular space or place? Is it a section diagram, a floor plan, an elevation drawing, a story, an anecdote?" (Brooks 1990: 157).

Working without a formula, the process is both inclusive and exclusive. Users cannot be provided with all the answers. "The books are primarily about questions, not about answers. Answers are based on obtaining information. Questions derive from what you knew in the first place" (Brooks 1990, 157). Discovery is accomplished by an erudite

Finally a world class guide constructed like the city itself! **ACCESS**PRESS *presents the city in geographical order. Brilliantly designed and easy to read, the form of the book follows the form of the city, providing instant orientation and an historical explanation of Paris's magical boulevards and avenues. Feast at ★★ & ★★★ restaurants, wine bars & cafes. Shop at bountiful boutiques and browse unique galleries. Stay at cozy comfortable or luxurious landmark hotels. View museums through the connoisseur's infallible eyes. A plethora of specially created maps, illustrations & lists of celebrities' personal favorites unveil Paris's deepest hidden treasures. This guide is as fascinating to read in an armchair before your trip as it is extraordinarily useful to carry in your pocket as you* **ACCESS** *the exotic theater of Paris from this unequalled backstage view.*

Finally a world class guide constructed like the city itself! **ACCESS**PRESS *presents the city in geographical order. Brilliantly designed and easy to read, the form of the book follows the form of the city, providing instant orientation and an historical explanation of Rome's magical piazzas and promenades. Feast at ★★★ & ★★★ restaurants, wine bars & trattorias. Shop at bountiful boutiques and browse unique galleries. Stay at cozy comfortable or luxurious landmark hotels. View museums through the connoisseur's infallible eyes. A plethora of specially created maps, illustrations & lists of celebrities' personal favorites unveil Rome's deepest hidden treasures. This guide is as fascinating to read in an armchair before your trip as it is extraordinarily useful to carry in your pocket as you* **ACCESS** *the exotic theater of Rome from this unequalled backstage view.*

Finally, books that look at cities the way tourists do – block by block... **ACCESS** *may be the best series for the chronically lost.*

— USA Today

Guidebooks from a genius: you'll be happy to learn that the finest guidebooks written, drawn and typeset in the last-well-half century are coming from architect-cartographer Richard Saul Wurman & **ACCESS**PRESS.

— Travel & Leisure Magazine

4-19.

Richard Saul Wurman and the staff of Access Press. The covers of Access Guides to Paris, Rome, and San Francisco. Dozens of guides have been completed, joined on the Access backlist by guides to sporting events, the *Wall Street Journal*, the Museum of Modern Art, the contemporary office, corporations, conferences, medicine, and the *Pacific Yellow Pages*. Wurman recognizes that, in the information age, information is where you find it—everywhere.

selection of images, facts, and intimations.

Information design has a pragmatic and a societal purpose. Whether providing geographic directions or furnishing data regarding joblessness, the graphic must convey the message as clearly and quickly as possible. Unlike the poster or magazine, information design must be functionally objective. Wurman's primary concern is the relational process of moving information from the page to the reader. "Form follows function" is not, to use graphic designer Joel Katz's phrase, "appearance-intensive." Style is sacrificed, as necessary, to provide product. Typography is firmly established in the iconography of an international style. Criticized as overly simplistic, even spartan, the demeanor of this information design discloses no allegiance to computer fashion.

Turning data into information is accomplished, however, with every means available. Accepting the advantages of technology, Wurman remains the only essential ingredient, the architect of the process. Once questions have begun to be answered, however, we are definitively dealing with computer design. Wurman uses the computer exclusively to choreograph data. At The Understanding Business, drafting tables are nonexistent—they have been displaced by several dozen Macintosh workstations.

Wurman's projects have recently moved in several directions beyond geography. He is in the process of completing the last of a planned trilogy containing his thoughts and recommendations for survival

in the information age. *Information Anxiety,* published by Doubleday in 1989, and *Understanding Understanding: The Structure of Instructions,* 1991, will be followed by *Learning Is Remembering What You're Interested In.* Access Press projects have included handbooks to football and Olympic games, the redesign of *TV Guide,* and the design and organization of "TED" (1984), "TED2" (1989), and "TED3" (1992), conferences in Technology/Entertainment/Design. Nicholas Negroponte, Herbie Hancock (playing his compositions for synthesizers), and Takenobu Igarashi have been among the luminaries featured at the multidisciplinary happenings.

Medical Access examines the human body, explains common medical tests, and provides data regarding the annual number of specific procedures, including time required to perform, recovery time, and costs. A guide to reading the *Wall Street Journal* has sold over 350,000 copies. *Office Access,* produced for Steelcase, provides aid in designing or redesigning the interior workspace. *Polaroid Access,* a gift to company employees, was commissioned to commemorate the firm's fiftieth anniversary.

The 1988 *Pacific Bell Smart Pages* is a particularly inventive collection of subject search pages, iconic pointers, lists of services and restaurants open twenty-four hours, and community access pages. The contents have been organized to fit human, rather than alphabetic, patterns. In the subject search pages, a main category (such as Automotive

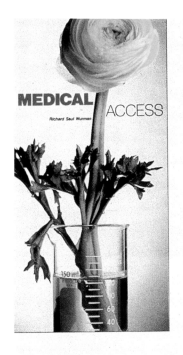

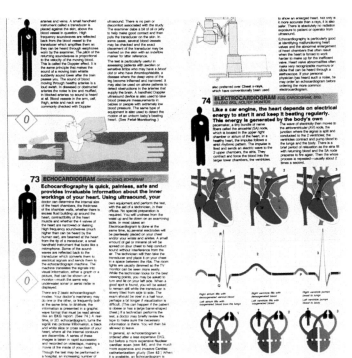

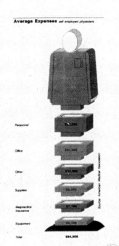

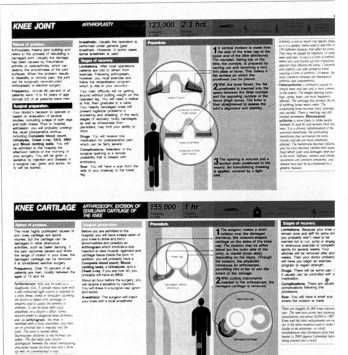

4-20.

Richard Saul Wurman and the staff of Access Press. Cover, chart, and two sample pages. *Medical Access*, 1985.

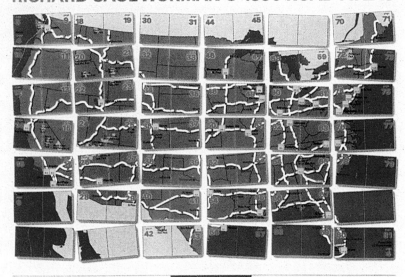

THE SMARTEST DISTANCE BETWEEN TWO POINTS

USATLAS

RICHARD SAUL WURMAN'S 1990 ROAD ATLAS

ACCESS PRESS

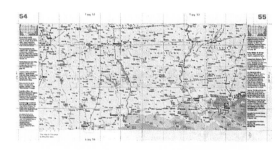

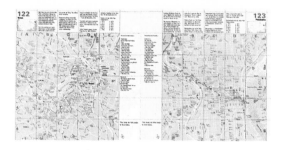

4–21.
Richard Saul Wurman and the staff of Access Press. *US Road Atlas 1990.* Developed at The Understanding Business, the Access Press office in San Francisco, the Atlas provides maps in three different scales: 250 square miles, twenty-five square miles, and five square miles. The Atlas is not organized in the traditional alphabetic, state-by-state fashion. Rather, as the traveller uses the map, a consecutive, interactive geography can be created. The Atlas user chooses blocked and number territories as required. The stratagem has been adopted by other map manufacturers. Each block map of The Atlas includes parenthetic information regarding the places and peoples being represented.

or Medical) is followed by subclassifications (Accidents, Emergencies, Repair, Trucks, etc.). The cartography, research, editing, and production for the now-familiar and very successful project were all completed at The Understanding Business.

In the Access Press *US Road Atlas 1990*, a joint publication with Prentice-Hall, a similar approach is used. As different map blocks are selected, the traveller is informally directed by apparently random, layered information that accompanies the precise directions of a well-ordered map. Layering is simplified by the computer. The designer can move about the page displayed on screen, visualizing possibility at a much more rapid rate than previously imaginable. Without this technology, imagining how layers of information might work is a very difficult process. Intellectually connecting and reconnecting parts of a multidimensional page requires genius. Few graphic designers could accomplish the task; still fewer information designers, who must be concerned with the maintenance of objectivity.

The technology permits visualization, previously an intellectual process, to occur on screen. The information designer is therefore able to predetermine whether substance is sacrificed to form. These are profound new abilities. What had formerly been brilliant could now be accomplished with a machine. That contribution has fostered interest that shows no signs of diminution.

To include the work of Skolos/Wedell in a chapter entitled "Hidden Machines" is to appear to be either blind or stupid. The firm was established in 1979, and its innovative work is obviously infused with technology. Though to use the word "hidden" is to stretch the point, the work of this firm is in no way driven by any exterior mechanism. One has the intense feeling that if the computer were eliminated from our collective consciousness tomorrow, Skolos/Wedell would discover a way to produce graphics much the same as before. No machine makes these images. The principals are responsible. Since they created such work before, they could create such images again, without the computer. It is this strange sense of "hidden" that applies to the firm—as with Lance Hidy, the computer is invisible because it is not needed. Indeed, though the aesthetic is relentlessly technological, the computer is actually used less often than it appears to be.

Nancy Skolos, Thomas Wedell, and Kenneth Raynor (who left the firm, previously known as Skolos, Wedell + Raynor, in 1990) each graduated from the Cranbook Academy of Art in the late 1970s. Skolos was educated as a graphic designer; Wedell and Raynor completed the course in photography. Along with Doublespace and Lucille Tenazas, they are among the leading proponents of a structured Cranbrook approach that formed an important basis of American Postmodernism. Skolos, who completed her education with graduate work at Yale University, has recently participated in the creation of a new design school. While explaining his reasons for joining that venture, Thomas Wedell begins a definition of the firm's response to computer graphic design: "We've joined with others in Boston to form the New School of Design. It will teach the basics that have been forgotten as we've used computers" (Parker 1990, 87). The computer can be an impediment. Skolos continues to use a sketch pad: "I work really intuitively on the level of a thumbnail sketch and try to keep it from losing its magic as much as I can" (Aldersey-Williams 1988, 147). Once converted to the computer screen, the ideas become so complex they could not be brought to their final form by hand. The resulting relationship is creatively healthy. While conceptually independent of the computer, Skolos has exploited its possibilities.

Katherine McCoy, chair of the Cranbrook Design Department, has argued that a new term, "digital graphic design," should replace existing phrases defining the graphic designer's use of the computer. "This is a new area that combines many traditional design skills in graphic design and design methodology with a whole new universe which is largely conceptual, rather than tangible" (McCoy 1991, 8). Skolos/Wedell actively understands that the prospects provided by the computer are extensions of previous possibility. The firm's principals have effectively presaged computer graphic design with a form based on mechano-technological potential. The escape from the

FONTS print

Leading the e
are not only breaking
aesthetic print quality for
crisp. But today's business o
the quality of each printed page
symbolize the high standards, pro
leadership, and financial strength be
the quality of each printed page is a function
Leading the electronic revolution in printing, tod
are not only breaking the barriers of speed and re
sthetic print quality for computer-generated output

g, today's ion page printers
d and reliability, they are a
d output. Yes
n me   egibility. B
ora   mage. It sh
ality   asmansh
on.   e sim
al t   des
ir,
d

horizontal plane was accomplished in traditional time. Computer time assists the activity; it is not sufficient in itself.

Reflections, shadows, and layered imagery create an effect that is both postmodern and metaphysical. Metallic cones and pyramids, photographic texture and condensed type suggest architectural motifs in hyperspace. The whimsical typographic ornamentation of Dutch graphic design is borrowed, floating about space, enforcing and reinforcing multidimensionality. In the most important work of the firm, the technological effects, whether created by the photographer, the designer, or with the aid of the computer, achieve drama and wonder. Communication becomes a puzzle, an exercise in audience participation. A collection of promotional pieces for Berkeley Typographics is typical of early work completed without computer aid. The search for dimension has recently been logically extended toward projects in interior design.

Skolos/Wedell first expropriated and then expanded on the Cranbrook/American Postmodern interest in technological effect and historic interest. Using the work of the surrealists as the basis of several projects, the firm has pursued an interest in intuition, illusion, and personal symbolism. A poster for Digital Equipment Corporation features a nautilus floating in a Magritte universe where gravity does not apply. In producing such projects, the firm employed several cameras, multidimensional models, Mylar, and startling perspectives provided by photographers Wedell and Raynor.

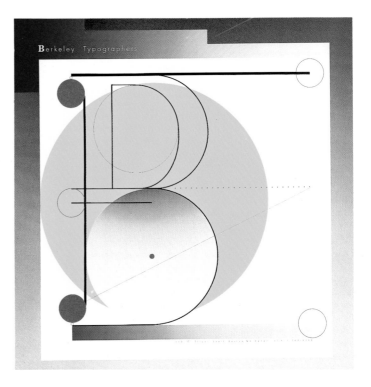

4-22.

(*previous page*) Skolos/Wedell. Poster for Delphax Systems, a manufacturer of high-speed ion page printers. The Cranbrook layering in black, red, and gray is accompanied by an unusual copper and black duotone. Nancy Skolos, designer; Thomas Wedell and Kenneth Raynor, photographers.

4-23.

Skolos/Wedell. Poster, Berkeley Typographers. The first poster in the series. Stylized geometry was a consistent motif of the firm prior to and after the introduction of the computer. Nancy Skolos, designer. 1984.

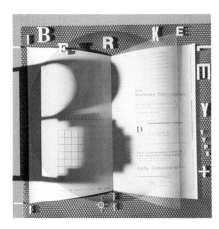

4-24.

Skolos/Wedell. Poster, third in the series, Berkeley Typographers. The image asserts the studio's pursuit of multidimensionality through overlapping screens. The telecommunications sales message is expertly conveyed in a computer graphic reflecting the *Emigre*/primitive/Punk aesthetic and Cranbrook training. Nancy Skolos, designer; Thomas Wedell and Kenneth Raynor, photographers.

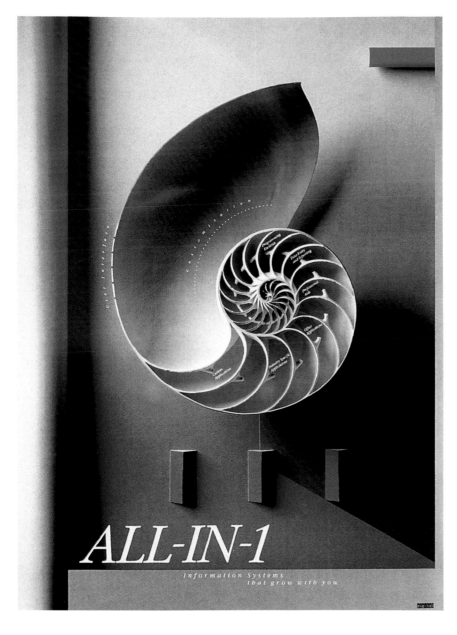

4-25.

Skolos/Wedell. *All-In-1 Information Systems that grow with you.* Poster for Digital Equipment Corporation. Technological grace is achieved through the perfection of shell, a signature typographic arc, and a radial image appropriate for a computer manufacturer emphasizing growth. Nancy Skolos, designer, for Innovision. Thomas Wedell, photographer. 1983.

4-26.

(*next page*) Skolos/Wedell. Poster for Laserscan, a color separations house. The "thrilling" degree of control provided by the Quantel Paintbox permitted this experimentation in computer depth. Thomas Wedell and Nancy Skolos, designers; Thomas Wedell and Kenneth Raynor, photographers. 1989.

A

TECHNICAL

NIGHTMARE

BROUGHT TO YOU BY

LASERSCAN

Photography and Design: Thomas Wedell and Nancy Skolos, Wedell + Raynor, Inc, 1988   Paintbox Designer: Yu Ling Wang, Laserscan, Inc.

Escaping the plane is made simpler via the computer. "We no longer have to set up several cameras to achieve the effect. Nor do we have to spend hours. . . . We simply take our transparencies to the Quantel and manipulate them" (Parker 1990, 87). Control of the imagescape is constant. Cubes, spheres, and cones are used because the appropriate degree of illusion can best be invoked in a geometric environment.

Skolos/Wedell has insisted on completing its own production work. Computer production was only grudgingly considered after the firm's independent quality standards were met. After that acceptance, Wedell continues to recognize that the computer cannot replace the indispensable human factor: "Even the Quantel can't give you the natural lighting you need to create a mood or effect. And if it does eventually, you will still need a person" (Parker 1990, 87).

A poster for Laserscan, a color separations house, was conceived after the firm adopted the use of the computer. The Macintosh, Freehand, Aldus Pagemaker, and Quantel Paintbox enabled the density and complexity of surrealist-inspired imagery. The continuous search to stay beyond the attempts of imitators is not narcissistic; there is a genuine commitment to extend capabilities and interests. This speculative attitude has necessitated a near-constant search for new expressive capabilities. Raynor explains that "just as we have pushed design to its limits, we are now pushing software to and beyond its limits" (Parker 1990, 84).

Conspicuously placed in the role of communicators on the edge, Skolos/Wedell maintain that they may be the "last of the Renaissance designers." Renaissance painters came to understand the world in three dimensions. The discovery of perspective was the underpinning of a new painterly style. Viewing the world as multifaceted, Skolos/Wedell designs to reflect the perspective of the people for whom they design.

Computer graphic designers are discovering new perspectival laws. Rather than the last of the old order, this firm may be among the first participating in a new renaissance. Skolos/Wedell reflects a new perspective being generated throughout the world. Some designers permit, even require, the active participation of the viewer in the process of discovering visual and intellectual novelty. For Skolos/Wedell, the computer is as incidental to that discovery as the brush in the hand of Flemish masters. This work is not done in the computer but, as Lance Hidy has expressed it, in the hearts and minds of the designer.

The machine is hidden by the heart. "The computer is used as an enabling tool while avoiding the cliche forms of obvious computer-generated design" (Hiebert, 1992). A book describes, at best, the particular design form of the moment. This is an artificial structure, an instrument groping toward the future, saying this is the way it was, and this is the way it may be. It is difficult to place, to effortlessly organize, the work of those who have personally redirected design and continue to do so. Some are more easily placed within the artifice. But April Greiman is visible and invisible, primitive and sophisticate, New Wave and postmodern. A new term, "hybrid imagery," has been created to avoid the artificial name-tag that diminishes a designer's work. To identify the consequential is easy. Classification is the difficulty. For the learners and the seekers, bearings change, making it difficult for the chronicler to neatly pin down the profound.

Kenneth Hiebert creates problems for us. As with Skolos/Wedell, we know he belongs, but we do not know quite where. His place is a new one—it is his own, not yet classified.

Hiebert's design resonates as personal expression. Conceding for the moment that technology is significant enough to assist creation, the computer is not actually hidden in Hiebert's work. It is separated by the unique independence of the individual. "The future of design is beyond preconception. . . . I am prevented by my philosophy from repeating history" (Hiebert 1992, 8). We can identify,

however, when history has been made. The founding chairman of graphic design at the University of the Arts (formerly the Philadelphia College of Art [PCA]), Hiebert began his association with the University of the Arts in 1966. In the 1970s, he assembled a faculty that included Greiman, Steff Geissbuhler, and William Longhauser. The program was the most significant sponsor of the American New Wave. Joining several other globally consequential schools, the University continues to inform the future of graphic design.

After completing studies at Gustavus Adolphus College and Bethel College, Hiebert entered the Allgemeine Kunstgewerbeschule in Basel and studied under Wolfgang Weingart and Armin Hoffman. Receiving the Swiss National Diploma in Design in 1964, he returned to the United States and taught at Carnegie-Mellon University, Yale University, and PCA. His connection to Basel and its approach is uninterrupted. Just as theory is often misunderstood by those who do not read it, the Basel approach is often misrepresented by those who have not experienced it. In creating the design program at the University of the Arts, Hiebert followed "guidelines" offered by Weingart: "It is important that school maintains an experimental character. The student should not be given irrevocable knowledge or values, but instead, the opportunity to independently search for such values and knowledge, to develop them, and learn to apply them" (Hiebert 1992, 8). Accepting such thinking as his credo, Hiebert has received awards for both his graphic

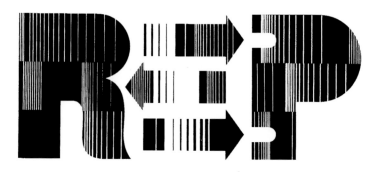

4-27.
Kenneth Hiebert.
Logotype: "REP." Symbol
created for a center for
planning, design, and
construction. 1972.

4-28.
Kenneth Hiebert.
Logotype. Demonstrating
the influence of
Weingartian studies in
prepress possibility, the
symbol represents a
guidebook used by
architects and builders
to locate factory
representatives. The
process camera, halftone
screen, repeated line,
apparently random
placement, and geometric
configuration were
standard contributors
to a vocabulary that, in
several years, was to be
popularized as New Wave.
The graphic is visibly
founded on underlying
structure. 1972.

design and his teaching, including the 1991 Master Teacher Award of the Graphic Design Education Association.

In 1989, Hiebert was the recipient of an individual design arts award from the National Endowment for the Arts. The grant allowed him to complete the research necessary to produce *Graphic Design Processes . . . universal to Unique,* published by Van Nostrand Reinhold in 1992. The documentation of the design process was completed with the extensive use of electronic media and the computer. *Graphic Design Processes* is a description of both a major research effort and a design philosophy. This specific exploration cannot be replicated (and cannot be adequately demonstrated here). It can and should serve as a model for honest investigators who follow. Just as his own education at Basel prepared him to meet the new (including the technological), a knowledge of Hiebert's examination should be standard equipment for the computer graphic designer.

As Hiebert has pointed out, it is surprising, and perhaps ironic, that his earlier work is at times more technical in appearance than his computer graphic design. In the early 1970s, he continued to refine his approach. A 1974 poster for Matrix, a service organization, exhibits an understanding of the Basel demand for underlying structure. "Structures exist. They are the undergirding of all communications whether or not they are named. . . . A knowledge of structure leads to connectedness of knowledge, and connectedness leads to intuition, because the pathways

4-29.

Kenneth Hiebert. *We are all bound together.* Poster for Matrix, a service organization. In a design universe solidly framed by Swiss Internationalism, diagonal type and wide letterspacing were quite unusual. The obvious diagonal grid is interrupted by typography and the integration of type and image. 1974.

4-30.

Kenneth Hiebert. Bulletin
Cover, Philadelphia
College of Art. An early
example of a conceit later
popularized: sans serif
typography set in a
distinctly non—
International style
manner. As the viewer
considers different
possibilities, the image
changes in terms of
both structure and
meaning. 1972.

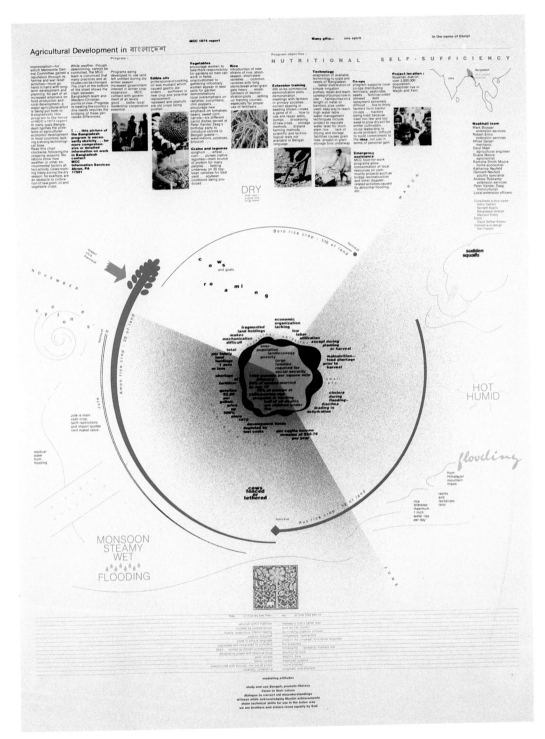

4-31.

Kenneth Hiebert. *Agricultural Development,* for Mennonite Central Committee. Graphic from report showing the interrelationship between crop and weather cycles and human need in Bangladesh. Type groupings were composed using the Mergenthaler VIP typesetter. Wolfgang Weingart recognized that this language became a formula by the 1980s: "I counted the cliches once when I was judging a competition. . . . I found about twenty." (Labuz 1990, 20). This institutionalization compelled Philip Meggs to name the plethora of copyists the "New Academy." Many phrases in this remarkable image were later plagiarized with abandon. Evocative spot drawings, information bands, hand lettering, diagonal type, wide letterspacing, geometric shapes as illustrative devices, shifting baselines, and floating typography are among the elements appropriated by those not following Hiebert's admonition to begin with one's own perception. Later devolving into visual cliches, the phrases are here employed with clear and cogent purpose. 1975.

are open" (Hiebert 1992, 16–17). Hiebert is among the minority of graphic designers who fully comprehend the expansive power of the grid. "Structure and meaning are permissions rather than constraints" (Hiebert 1992, 22). "Structure releases energy and thought while giving direction" (Hiebert 1992, 23). Throughout the 1970s, with his colleagues at PCA, Hiebert moved away from an International Style which venerated obvious pattern. Though the resulting organization was less dependent and less conspicuous, the grid remained the hidden organizational principle.

In its purest form, the complaint of the new aesthetic was not against the grid, but against the imposition of particular order. In 1973, Weingart delivered a series of lectures at American design schools and the revolt was well underway. A cover design of the period, a bulletin for PCA, is an interesting comment on the ways one might look at the world. There is no "right" way of looking at the image. Turned one way, typography is upside down; when a photograph of walking people is turned in a certain way, we focus on the shadows of the walkers rather than on the individuals themselves. The incorporation of four simple design elements (a photograph and three pieces of typography) invokes basic questions regarding vision and design. A far more complicated set of elements, and an increasingly radical approach, is employed in a graphic prepared for a 1975 report. Recognizing that structure can be monotonous, Hiebert underlines the importance of the human individual as interactive

participant in the viewing process. "A good structure defines a program for gaining intimacy" (Hiebert 1988, 8). The structuralist approach, in the right hands and heart, provides a visual grammar that reaches people and creates understanding.

In the 1970s and 1980s, Hiebert continued to develop his own style and the vision of his students. His participation in an experimental analysis of computerized typesetting as a Research Associate at Yale and his interest in multidimensional, sight-and-sound composition were in keeping with his training as a Basel designer. A 1983 poster announcing a lecture at PCA is representative. New elements had been introduced and were rapidly becoming popular. Torn paper, large individual letters, halftone screens, fragments of cut typography, and dashes of paint joined an earlier arsenal of effects.

From a powerful base of established form and process, Hiebert was well prepared, in 1988, to begin to master the computer. His experiments with the Apple Macintosh, the Apple Scanner, MacVision video digitizing software, and the LaserWriter could not be called complete. They are still continuing. However, his description of his learning, *Graphic Design Processes . . . universal to Unique,* was begun in the fall of 1988 and completed in May 1991. The kinetic options available to either the computer user or a person browsing through a book cannot be replicated. In this case, it is impossible to understand the thought behind the image without reading, or at least having available,

April Greiman

presented by the
Graphic Design Department
of the Philadelphia
College of Art
and AIGA/Philadelphia

13

Visual-aural performance, two design demonstrations and discussion

8:00 p.m. Tuesday, March 13, 1984

CBS Auditorium and Great Hall
Philadelphia College of Art, Broad and Pine Entrance

Information (215) 893-3134

PCA students and faculty free,
other students with ID $2,
AIGA/Philadelphia members free,
non-members $5.

the whole image. A glimpse of several graphics must suffice.

This inquiry was begun by a successful graphic designer with an enviable record. His involvement with the computer was fueled not by economics or self-interest but by his own questions regarding the medium and its role in visual communication. For Hiebert, the computer does not direct graphic design. It empowers the designer, permitting a greater, and perhaps faster, development of the individual communicator. Le Corbusier is quoted: "Creation is a patient search." Every project, whether an illuminated book or an interactive video, is founded on basic principles not quickly or easily understood. After the foundation is laid, technology may expedite, and relieve, the arduous play of ideation. Greater nuances of possibility are available. Though occurring more rapidly, the probing mechanism—determining value, rejecting one route, accepting another, moving toward unexpected solutions—does not change.

In moving from one medium to another, we expect continuity. Several of Hiebert's sketches for a logotype are a case in point. Related to a symbol created in 1972, these ideas are not found in the computer. Assistance is the most that is expected. Moreover, aid and comfort can be prescribed only to those knowledgeable enough to understand the cure.

Pages from *Graphic Design Processes* reveal experiments in several levels of multidimensionality: intellectual, visual, chro-

4-32.

Kenneth Hiebert. *Made in Space.* Poster announcing a presentation by April Greiman, co-sponsored by the Graphic Design Department of the Philadelphia College of Art and by American Institute of Graphic Arts (AIGA), Philadelphia. 1983 (opposite).

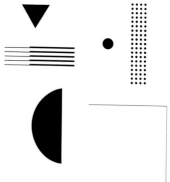

4-33.

Kenneth Hiebert. Sketch for a logotype. The client is the journal, *Communication Theory.* In a personal letter, Hiebert reports a new problem for the new computer designer: "The dilemma in showing, for example, the logo exploration for *Communication Theory* is that the computer enables looking at far more options and nuances than before. The studies would make a book in their own right; these are just a few of the sketches" (Hiebert 1991, personal letter). Drawn on the Macintosh. 1990.

4-34.

Kenneth Hiebert. The parts of the vocabulary created for the design of the logotype, available to the graphic designer for reconfiguration. Logotype sketches for journal, *Communication Theory* 1990 (see next page).

matic, and creative. The third chapter, "Word to Image," is a visual fugue on the theme of a broken unbreakable cup. Twenty-four alternatives/steps/chances/opportunities were selected and discussed. After six distinct goals are established, MacVision, Digital Darkroom, Aldus FreeHand, the Macintosh, and Hiebert's vision were used to explore the word/picture relationship. The form of the penultimate design is an expression of chaos within structure.

In the next chapter, "Texture :: Pattern," the computer is used to explore the vernacular patterns of the Oaxaca Valley, Mexico. The process began with a study trip. A notation system was created by trial and error at the first site—it consisted of perspective drawings, rubbings, and several chance factors. Patterns were discovered and later scanned. Forty-eight distinct patterns were identified and sorted with Aldus PageMaker and Canvas. "These forms stimulate probes into fresh combinations, suggesting new potential for graphic expression" (Hiebert 1992, 105). A type font was created based on the lettering used to make notations. The goals of this project were achieved: "To use a travel experience as a means of renewal. . . . To create a useful program of registering visual impressions. . . . To allow for chance factors to affect choices. . . . To experiment freely with new visual material." (Hiebert 1992, 106). Though accelerating the accomplishment, the computer is incidental to the process of discovery.

That is not necessarily the case with

4-35.
Kenneth Hiebert. Several alternative configurations of the vocabulary. Logotype sketches for journal. *Communication Theory*. 1990 (opposite).

4-36.
Kenneth Hiebert. Page from *Graphic Design Processes*. Chapter 3. Word to Image. Project: The Unbreakable Cup. 1992.

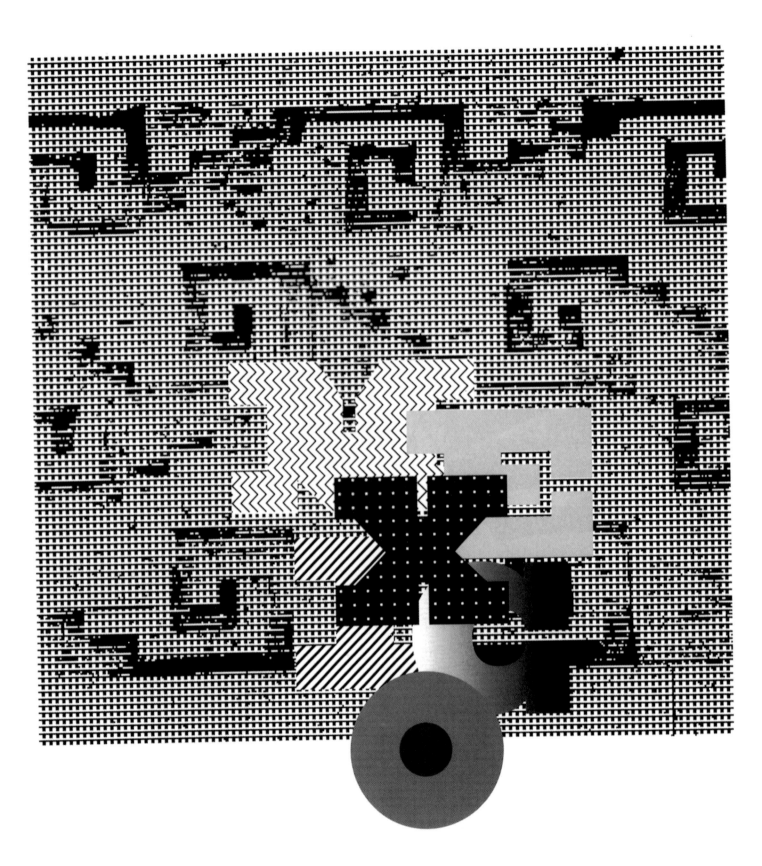

Hiebert's explorations of color. Using Aldus FreeHand exclusively, Hiebert creates a structure for understanding color interaction. From these experiments, a unique, triadic resonance is progressively developed and applied to a series of posters. Dozens of variations were attempted. That contribution, based on an ability to quickly order fresh color changes, was provided by computer speed. The final poster, a geometric collaboration of triangles, squares, and rectangles, seems a major distance from a 1974 poster anchored on a visible grid.

"The computer is a source for unpredictable shifts and transformations" (Hiebert 1992, 15). As a computer graphic designer, Hiebert has completed a personal, deep-space exploration of potential. The computer makes credible that which others could not consider, provoking "fresh insight into what is possible." But, Hiebert argues, only after receiving and understanding adequate direction will the designer be able to notice that which deserves attention. To label *Graphic Design Processes* a lesson book in computer graphic design would be a disservice. The book is a primer in the principles of graphic design, a philosophical expression, and an explanation of creative process. The computer plays a small but necessary role. Understanding that, Hiebert does not hide the computer. He transcends it. After spending a career educating his own students, he has performed the greater task of educating us all. Or, at least, those who are willing to be educated.

4-37.

Kenneth Hiebert. Page from *Graphic Design Processes*. Chapter 4. Texture :: Pattern. Project: Travel Notations and Utilization. 1992.

4-38.

Kenneth Hiebert. Page from *Graphic Design Processes*. Chapter 5. Color. Project: Universal/Unique Poster. Poster 3, probing the interaction of cool and warm colors. 1992.

4-39.

Kenneth Hiebert. Page from *Graphic Design Processes*. Chapter 5. Color. Project: Universal/Unique Poster. Poster 5, a further exploration in color relationships. 1992 (see next page).

AFTERWORD

The unifying factor joining the computer graphic designers discussed in this chapter has been vision. Even at Apple Creative Services, even before the computer, there was a conception of what design should do and be. In some cases, the vision has been stylistic; in others, prophetic. At times the two possibilities have merged.

Without announcement, each of these computer graphic designers has forged a means to use the computer invisibly. There is no special honor in doing so. But, confronted by the technology, they have provided an example most of us will follow. There is no doubt that the computer will be accepted. Perhaps irrationally, and without specific reason for believing so, it is easy to believe that the hidden machine will be the newest wave.

We wish to maintain the human quality of our communication. These designers have given us a means to achieve personal ends.

With its templates, typefaces, perfect circles, and unblemished (and unremarkable) typography, the computer erodes the need for traditional design skills. While we no longer need to use technical pen or T-square, we cannot lay aside the knowledge of mass, form, shape, and line habitually gained through the use of old tools.

New ways of learning and teaching must be mastered. Without craft, that proficiency all these designers bring to the computer, graphic design and graphic designers may suffer. Fortunately, whether hidden or not, the machine may be forced into service against itself. We have received lessons from computer graphic designers. These instructions provide us with paradigms that are instructions on how to learn. It is incumbent on us to remember that these are not prototypes. They are displays of vision that cannot be copied.

5

Computer graphic designers who have achieved a purposeful style prudently argue that they sense no need to transfigure themselves. To achieve discipline and then change for the sake of change is to be both ignorant and reckless. Graphic designers who have realized their own voice are neither. New means are nevertheless reasonably adopted, filling an already established vision.

An essentially reflective form, graphic design has rarely effected cultural change. In a global society filled with planners and futurists, the vehicle of the present is the computer. Recognizing that instrument's potential, computer graphic designers may participate, perhaps for the first time, in creating their own future. Juxtaposed on the poles of reaction and prediction, new creators are attempting to do so.

The designers discussed in this chapter have been formed by the postindustrial age. They are the purest users of the computer. If there is no connection to a past, there is also no reason to reject it: irrelevant paradigms are passively ignored. Reactions to a new stimulus provide these new archetypes. Each alludes, at the least, to a possible world, if not a possible future. "Computer technology promises to change the nature of design and participate in the establishment of new forms of graphic expression" (Nahin and Allmendinger 1985, 279). Understanding this potential, the visionary believes that the computer and the graphic designer must play an increasingly active role in redefining the values of a new civilization. Visionaries are unfortunately rare. We do not suffer their presence gladly. Goading us with unpleasant dreams of expectation and obligation, they are affably ignored.

Many have made the cogent claim that ignorance is not the best policy. The technology will not quietly go away. Indeed, it has permeated both our contemporary culture and, for the designers discussed in this chapter, every possible future. There are dangers in discussing possibilities. Noting that the messenger should not be held responsible by those who hesitate in looking forward, Muriel Cooper reminds us of the urgency of this change: "There is an inevitable Jekyll-Hyde syndrome that must be recognized and managed by us all. The changes that will be effected by the computer and the information revolution are pervasive. Every aspect of every profession and every life will be changed by it." (Cooper 1989, 30). Inevitably, there is also a responsibility in defining futures: "It is imperative that we all spend less time ignoring or challenging the threat of computers, and educate ourselves and par-

ticipate in the direction of this polymorphous medium." (Cooper 1989, 30)

Not all designers are oracles. Accepting or assigning that responsibility is precarious. It is unjust, moreover, to criticize communicators for failing in a role they did not presume. The visual remains the substance of graphic design. In this chapter, we see an aversion to the obvious, to pixelated form. Yet the definitive characteristic of this work remains elusive. Allusions often are.

These designers work without specific visual reference to the computer. Though the images do not proclaim themselves to be digital graphic design, these statements could not, and were not, made before the computer. This communication does not declare its dependence. This is not primitivism or the cultured computer. We often cannot identify this work as computer graphic design. For various reasons, it must be.

Several of these forms have developed without reliance on prior constructs. They need not be a visible rejection of the past. A more mature perspective has emerged. Postulating that technology is necessary to reflect the zeitgeist of this new age, visual and communicative potential is created. Structural and epistemic reliance join stylistic autonomy. Though the computer is invisible, these messages arrive only through and because of the machine.

Impact is differentially felt. Cultural lag, unavailability of technology, intellectual intransigence, or plain stubbornness may be the reasons. Outside of Japan and the United States, computer experimentation has yielded fewer models. Those that do exist tend to assume the role of design guerrilla fighter: Max Kisman, Rudy VanderLans, Zuzana Licko, Thunder Jockeys. Graham Elliot of Thunder Jockeys, on graphic designers: "many are scared of film and video because they've been taught by squares" (Aldersey-Williams 1989, 53). The world must be changed.

Recognizing the revolution, the princi pals of 8vo take a distinctive approach. In the mid-1980s, caught in the cauldron of British enthusiasm for the punk patterns of Neville Brody, Malcolm Garrett, and Terry Jones, 8vo consciously maintained modernist control. By 1987, Punk had been so blatantly pirated that it wasn't punk to do punk anymore. Brody joined the counterrevolutionary movement emphasizing the use of clarity and Helvetica. The equilibrium of a consistent approach meant that 8vo was unaffected by this activity. Having declared a point of view, they continued to develop, as they had done before. Now everyone else agreed with them.

Headed by Simon Johnston, Hamish Muir, Michael Burke, and Mark Holt, 8vo emphasizes typographic solutions and an experimental attitude. Personal expression is required, within constraints. Muir and Johnston, educated at the Allgemeine Kuntsgewerbeschule under Wolfgang Weingart, have acknowledged the perspective of the new Basel approach. Controlled experiments, an absence of illustration, and the structured approach of the grid are accepted as formal values. "I don't think modernism is a style, really. It's more like the truth. It's everything else that is wrong, and modernism the thing that's right. That *is* a fairly extreme view" (Aldersey-Williams 1989, 49). This view is often misunderstood. Agreeing with Weingart, Hiebert, and Greiman, Muir is arguing for a design process rather than for or against a particular design style. "During the first four years, we were laying the ground rules. Now we're breaking our own rules. But we had to have those rules to start with. It's a building process" (*Emigre 14,* 23). When the Basel approach (or any approach) to process is established, the individual is able to coherently develop. Without process there is chaos.

The studio's most visible product is *octavo: an international journal of typography.* Launched in 1986, the original intent of the firm was to produce eight issues to be published at intervals of six months. The journal is a proclamation of design intent, and a record of experimentation. The two issues of 1988 are representative of an interest in extending Muir's modernist tradition. Such extensions are built on both Basel and an existing 8vo style. The cover of *octavo 88.5* is a translucent flyleaf. Here are possibilities: typography may be easily read or appreciated as visual layering. The type printed on the cover is completely legible if the opacity (the flyleaf) is lifted. The interior pages are crisply designed, with diagonal columns of type joined by typographic illustrations and photographic reproductions.

In *octavo 88.6,* patterns become increasingly difficult to read. Type is printed on the front and the reverse of the flyleaf (figure 5-3). The text concerns the graphic designer's responsibility to environment and society. Phrases from the text: "We are all targets of the communication industry. Despite our increasing concern with environmental pollution, we are seemingly oblivious

5-1.

8vo. octavo 88-5. Editors: Simon Johnston, Mark Holt, Michael Burke, and Hamish Muir. Orange, green, black, and yellow on a translucent cover. The typography of the first interior page is visible below; legibility is sacrificed in the service of form. The diagonal typography and sans serif type are standard phrases in the Basel vocabulary. At the bottom of the orange information bar is the truncated phrase, "fifth of eight iss." A row of dots and the increasingly vibrant orange hue leads the viewer in the same direction as the phrase—inward toward the contents of the journal. 1988.

to visual pollution—the proliferation of signs, information and advertisements" (*octavo 88.6*). "This is disposable communication for a throw-away culture. . . . We are forced to look at them because they have become an integral and insidious part of our environment" (*octavo 88.6*).

The studio's professional commitment is shared by many designers who have recently come to understand the importance of disciplinary responsibility, social concern, ethics, history, and context. In this case, 8vo cannot be accused of adding clutter to the visible world. These multidimensional graphics require attention. The nature of 8vo's prediction for the future is clear: the computer graphic designer must take permanent responsibility for the care of our visual environment.

Although informational rather than evocative, the message is reminiscent of William Morris. Confronted by the earlier visual junk of Victoriana, Morris argued that the designer must use every possible stratagem to force the viewer to take the time to notice, to appreciate, and, finally, to comprehend. Similarly, 8vo captures the reader. Images demand attention. Once caught, we are able to discern substance for ourselves.

On the first spread of *octavo 88.6*, a video image accompanies the legend, "Signs of Revolution." The text discusses Robert Venturi's *Learning from Las Vegas* and the nature of signs. Several pages follow that begin a hyperspace journey into banks of

5-2.

8vo. *octavo 88-5*. Editors: Simon Johnson, Mark Holt, Michael Burke, and Hamish Muir. Typography in the interior spreads is quite legible. An interesting table of contents is joined by gradations of color. 1988.

5-3.

8vo. *octavo 88-6*. Editors: Simon Johnson, Mark Holt, Michael Burke, and Hamish Muir. The translucent cover contains a table of contents and the words, set on the reverse of the cover, "information environm sign." In each issue, the cover folds around the first page. Here the enfolded page contains a continuation of text begun on the first page, a page the reader has not yet read. The interactivity of *octavo* cover designs has been consistently developed. 1988.

5-4.

(*next page*) 8vo. *octavo 88-6*. Editors: Simon Johnson, Mark Holt, Michael Burke, and Hamish Muir. The first two-page spread. The recognition of a communication revolution is accompanied by the prototypical neon of Robert Venturi's image of Las Vegas. 1988.

information
environm
sign

In the contemporary environment we are besieged by a cacophony of words, signs and images, each directing, shouting and cajoling... we are all targets of the communication industry. Despite our increasing concern with environmental pollution, we are seemingly oblivious to visual pollution – the proliferation of signs, information and advertisements, which are often the clearest visible indicators of our continuing exploitation

8 Protest Time: An anthology of timetable typography by Barry Kitts examines the history of the timetable through its close links with the development of railways.

12 Highway Codes: An investigation by Neil Parker into the typefaces and coding conventions used... the idiosyncratic but intriguing field of vehicle registration plates.

AN ·349238

1 Signs of Revolution...

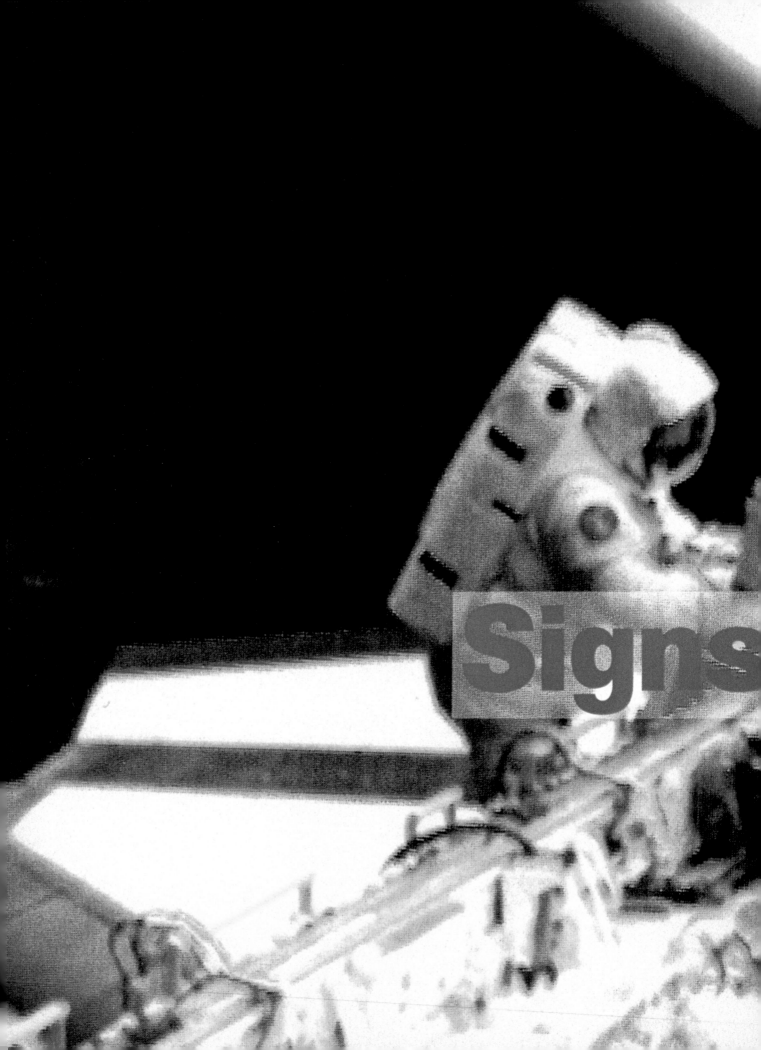

The language of architecture is under assault from the language of signs: Martin Pawley, architecture correspondent of *The Guardian*, argues that with the imperative of communication beginning to dominate our environment, we must reassess the changing relationship between signs and buildings.

# of Revolution

When in 1970 Robert Venturi and Denise Scott Brown first reported that architects could learn from Las Vegas, the city of signs, they were already too late. They discovered Las Vegas the way Columbus discovered America, by ignoring the natives and insisting that it was somewhere else when they got there.

Like most early explorers, Venturi and Scott Brown were not the first people, but only the first people of a certain type to stumble upon somewhere. The monstrous liquid seething krill signs of the gambling hell already hovered over a flourishing city when they got there. But unlike the rest of its population the Venturis were English-speaking academic architects. Amazed by these gigantic structures, as vast and inexplicable as Easter Island statues, the Venturis took possession of them in the name of architecture. 'There is a psychedelic and semiological drug overdose of a desert city in the West', they reported on their Lewis and Clark-like return to the East Coast, 'that could be beneficial to architects if it were taken in very small doses'. They themselves rapidly proved (by putting a gold imitation TV aerial on top of an old people's home) that tiny drops of the priceless hologram of semiological illumination could be used by any architect without apparent side effects. In the liberal climate of the early 70s this seemed alright. Only three years before, the magazine *Progressive Architecture* had sponsored experiments during which the subjects designed buildings while under the influence of lysergamides. This was the same sort of thing. The new consciousness. It wouldn't be the end of the art. Like Main Street, if not marijuana, forests of signs were 'almost alright'. The Venturis called their book 'Learning from Las Vegas'.

colored information bars. This tendency would be broadened in later issues of the journal.

By 1990, the 8vo connection to computer graphic design had been established. The issue begins with a dramatic suggestion: *the new synthesis* is far more than a titular change. Confronted by the computer, 8vo does not abandon modernist process. The grid is still identifiable. But these graphics are remarkably different than those that preceded. A new need is forcefully proclaimed on the flyleaf interior: "A new language of synthesis is needed. . . . It must challenge the hierarchy of romantic pastiche. The new synthesis must express the relationship between the meaning and appearance of type and image while pushing the frontiers of the new technology; using structure and gestalt to go further than the "it's done on the computer; it must be amazing pictorial typo-wallpaper of today" (*octavo 90-7*).

8vo believes that the computer forces the graphic designer into the new. Technology and the means of production determine form. When these determinants are new, radical change must occur from within. Sans serif typefaces, Muir contends, are "no longer relevant in an age of desktop publishing and laser-setting. We must find a vocabulary of expression that has meaning today" (*octavo 90-7*).

That vocabulary is based on a structured approach and the recognition that the problem is decidedly ours. Spurning "letterpress-derived-dead-typography . . . and not

just print—newspapers, books and magazines, it's *everything,* from vdus through tv titles to electronic information systems" (*octavo 90-7*) is a declaration not remarkably dissimilar from that of Weingart's rejection of Swiss formalism. In nine interior two-page spreads, the flyleaf, and the cover, a grid is actually printed on the page. Used earlier as a visual pun by those who rejected the grid entirely, here the visual phrase of the grid acknowledges a heritage. Though the structure is still relevant, it is not clear whether the modernist inheritance is as warmly accepted.

The most significant interior spread in *octavo 90-7* is a discussion of visual literacy. The form is associated with both Basel and the objective Zurich Style of Seigfried Odertmatt and Rosmarie Tissi. The spontaneity, playfulness, and palette of the Odermatt & Tissi typographic collage are echoed in a colorful collection of imprinted grids, horizontal sans serifs, and incongruously numbered labels. Now produced entirely with the computer, the design is a commentary on communication problems in an age of information and, not parenthetically, a criticism of graphic designers who react (and rob) but do not read. "Most people who buy *Octavo* do not read it . . . they are preconditioned to respond to type as image rather than as type and image. So much for visual literacy!" (*octavo 90.7*) The new synthesis is a way out of this quandary.

Computer graphic design is essentially multidimensional and interactive. 8vo believes

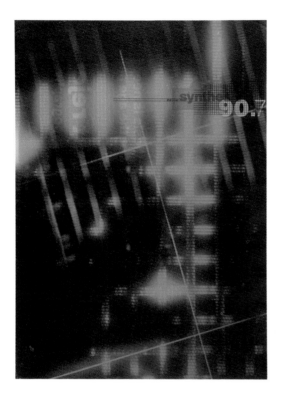

5-5.

8vo. *octavo 90-7*. Designed and edited by Mark Holt, Hamish Muir, and Michael Burke. Flyleaf of the issue, *the new synthesis*. Typography is printed in red, black, and white. The translucent flyleaf is printed on a base of black, thus preventing the reader from viewing the cover. The grid is the predominant image of the issue, seen here and on the cover as an amorphous pattern of square cells. In the interior spreads, a collection of nine different yellow grids are impressed on the page. 1990.

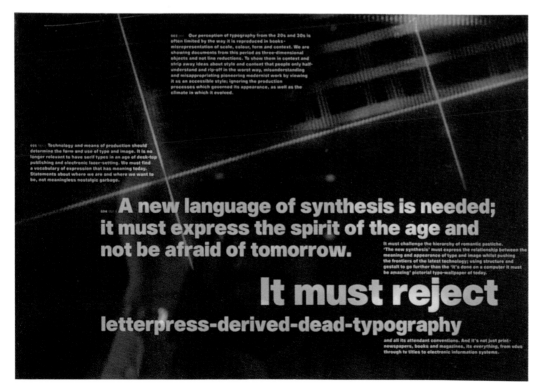

5-6.

8vo. *octavo 90-7*. Designed and edited by Mark Holt, Hamish Muir, and Michael Burke. The interior flyleaf, front. The new synthesis is defined both visually and verbally. 1990.

5-7.

8vo. octavo 90-7.
Designed and edited by
Mark Holt, Hamish Muir,
and Michael Burke. The
cover. Repeated cells are
joined by an eye, icon of
vision. 1990.

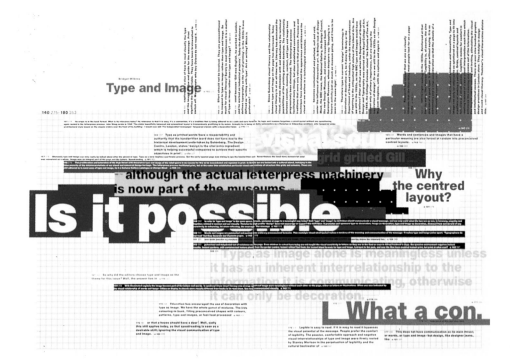

5-8.

8vo. octavo 90-7.
Designed and edited by
Mark Holt, Hamish Muir,
and Michael Burke.
Interior spread. The
connection to Odermatt &
Tissi presents an
opportunity for multiple
levels of understanding.
The central problem of the
issue is found in several
epigrammatic statements:
"Most people who buy
Octavo do not read it,"
"how much of this you
have read," "What a con,"
and "Typographers do not
read." The text, set in
disconnected sections, is
quite difficult to follow.
Obviously believing that
their audience must be
forced to read, the puzzle
of these pages is a visual
invitation to read while
looking at the pictures.
(The same issue has
recently been discussed in
*Emigre I5: Do You Read
Me?*) The complete text is
contained, in traditional
linear manner, at the
back of *octavo 90.7.* 1990.

that those attributes *must* be exploited. The basic function and purpose of graphic design, to communicate, must be reestablished. "There are over nine-hundred graphic design practices in London alone. They indulge in design and numb visual literacy" (*octavo 90.7*). Neglected by designers who concentrate on form without substance, lost in the myriad of dizzying signs, prepared using outmoded tools, communication has suffered. The essentially human discourse provided by the graphic designer slowly fades.

We have not yet learned to adapt to a technological revolution. Engaging a battle against several forms of visual illiteracy, new design—based in the synthesis of structure and technology—is required. 8vo believes our only serviceable weapons will be those created by new tools.

There are other battles to be fought, not the least of which is creating a recognizable vision in the blur of the mediascape. 8vo's achievement is a remarkable example of poststructuralist revisionism. A philosophical foundation, however, is not an invariable investment of the computer graphic designer. Others have taken a more traditional approach to forge a personal style.

The task is complicated by the rapidity with which originality is absorbed by counterfeiters. In a design universe driven by nanosecond time, creativity is more difficult to discover and maintain. Even before reputations are made, they seem to be copied. In this climate, any individual achievement is remarkable.

In the case of The Johnee Bee Show, two factors have synergistically combined. First, Johnee Bee works from a studio in Irvine, California, placing himself squarely within an ethos of saturated pastels, Pacific Wave mood, Disney Land characterizations, and pop humor. Second, the illustrator and graphic designer is self-taught. After a stint as an apprentice to a photographer and retoucher, Johnee Bee discovered the computer. Because he maintains no allegiance to a specific program, his graphics display an intuitive voice. He is a designer only because he is a computer designer.

The graphics are not stylistically dependent on the computer. Sharp angles, absence of background space, punk cartoon characters, broad range of color, and retro imagery are computer constructions. Using the Macintosh and Adobe Illustrator 88, he is able to work quickly and efficiently, infusing spot drawings and more complicated illustrations with equal degrees of energy and humor.

A self-promotional piece is representative of a particularly Californian computer style. The perspective and geometry are somewhat confused. Believing that the clarity of a specific design school approach may be visually debilitating, Johnee Bee argues that confusion is simply a means to attract—and retain—interest. Typography is strewn about a page populated by scattered images from an old design vernacular. As the tools of the trade are figuratively and visually kicked from the studio, BitMan waits on the Macintosh screen. This cartoon character was created for Ingram Micro D, a software manufacturer and distributor. As BitMan moves around the country, attending exhibitions and conferences, Johnee Bee supplies images locating the character in the appropriate city. The sharp angles, drop shadows, original lettering, and color scheme are constituent phrases in a vocabulary stimulated by comix and the contrived imperfections of American Punk.

A different but related aesthetic is recoverable in retro-inspired illustrations. These reconstructions allude to a wide range of twentieth-century models. A brochure for Sun Computers features a heroic realist figure framed in a stylized medallion. The distance between System 7 Man and BitMan is

5-9.

The Johnee Bee Show. Spot drawing on the Macintosh: bear and bull. The Punk aesthetic is one of several influences the illustrator assumes to meet particular demands of the client and the illustration. Drawn with Adobe Illustrator. 1990.

5-10.

The Johnee Bee Show. Experimental spot drawing on the Macintosh. The juncture of constructivist principles and California pastels. Drawn with Adobe Illustrator. 1990.

not great. Each character is formed from solid fields, generalized anatomy, and strong chromatic contrasts. The muted colors are a valid choice within this aesthetic range. An interior illustration points to the unhesitatingly geometric basis of this design. A second illustration, a spot drawing alluding to the geometrically inspired Dubonnet man of A.M. Cassandre, is influenced by the Cubist conceits of the 1930s. Humor is a common theme in Johnee Bee's visual repertoire.

More elegant approaches to computer retro are taken. A brochure design for Page One, a typesetting service bureau, is an example. Continuing to demonstrate both a knowledge of design history and a fine illustrative sense, Johnee Bee proves that the comix connection is a decision rather than a given. Suggesting the American factory aesthetic expressed in Works Progress Administration (WPA) posters and the paintings and photography of Charles Sheeler, the composition is inspired by both pictorial modernism and heroic realism. We are also reminded of the architecture of contemporaneous Linotype linecasters, so significant in the "Page One" newspaper industry. The typography is far more graceful than the tortured calligraphy of Punk graphics. The omnipresent computer is not revealed.

When it would be antithetical to an historicist approach to do so, Johnee Bee does not disclose that he is among the first of a new generation. There will, increasingly, be those who will become designers *because* of the computer. For Johnee Bee, and for those who follow him, the computer need not be

5-11.

The Johnee Bee Show. *Get Out and Out.* Self-promotional poster distributed to clients. On the reverse is a calendar of upcoming computer events. The vernacular tools of the traditional designer include Rub A Dub It Type, Stinky Ink, and Wrong Color Markers. The pencil, triangle, drawing table, type book, and paint tube are evicted as well. Typographic baselines are easily manipulated with Adobe software. Type is imprinted with tricolor drop shadows (green, purple, and black). 1991.

5-12.

The Johnee Bee Show. *BitMan: The Great Mac-D-Caper IV.* The celebration in San Francisco color could have come from some place other than California. But it isn't very likely. The harsh geometry, drop shadows, type balloon, and severe perspective are phrases from the comix vocabulary. BitMan has experienced several incarnations in American cities hosting computer exhibitions and conventions. This "all-new adventure" takes place in San Francisco. 1990.

5-13.

The Johnee Bee Show. Spot drawing influenced by the pictorial modernism of the 1930s. The illustrator's comment on one facet of our new technology: "Or please press 782951 for the 12th Department of the 3rd product of our choice or. . . ." 1991.

5-14.

The Johnee Bee Show. *Page One*. Design for Page One, a Postscript service bureau featuring the Linotronic typesetter. A more elegant nature is typical of a second retro approach to computer illustration. 1990.

revealed. But it must be present. Because he is exclusively a computer artist, these illustrations and designs could not exist outside the computerized universe.

The computer has permitted an unschooled individual to create images with a difference. This is not remarkable in itself. Many major contributors, both in the recent past and today, have not studied graphic design at university. Several influential design educators have suggested that this might produce better educated (and therefore better) designers. But these are no longer theoretical musings. An individual with the ability to make wise aesthetic choices has proved able to develop several distinct computer styles.

Design is no longer a closed loop. We have proof, once again, that it is no longer necessary to discipline yourself, to participate in the academic discourse of graphic design, to become a graphic designer. Technology is truly democratic. Anyone can now invite themselves into our history. That allusion to a potential future is a revolution many do not wish to consider.

Cryptic messages and visual confusion seem to be the directives of the day. The message is actually not new. The power of these qualities were suggested in the 1960s by French poster designers Roman Cieslewicz and Grapus, the unique typographic lettrism of Robert Massin, and the psychedelic imagery of Wes Wilson and Victor Moscoso. The enigma of anonymity has intensified. Seeking to capture attention, computer graphic designers have learned to capitalize on randomness.

Great risks are being taken. In the conversation that is graphic design, learned control has been a means used to declare professional intent. Basing a style on chance jeopardizes both clarity and position. Happenstance makes it more difficult for the graphic designer to pronounce authority; the uneducated may be allowed full membership within this practice. As a tool, the computer makes it less possible to differentiate between layman and specialist.

Michael Weymouth Design of Boston provides solutions to corporate problems through *loss* of control, offered by the computer. "It's not super-organized Swiss-Bauhaus design. It's not controlled—it's more a controlled accident, like a watercolor. It takes advantage of whatever medium you're in, and it uses a whole palette of things totally contrary to the Swiss school" (S. D. Warren Company 1988, 34). By the late 1980s, visual debris had spread so widely that even the most staid of design responsibilities, the

annual report, was seeking attention among the junk. Exploiting the indiscriminate path of visual providence, Weymouth and Mara Kilnins intuitively capture the appropriate alternative. For the moment, unusual effects seize the day. It has become ever more difficult, of course, to be unusual. Intuitive energy, coincidence, and appreciation for serendipitous value are hard to maintain. Thus far, Weymouth Design has been able to discharge the responsibility.

A 1987 annual report for the Massachusetts Industrial Finance Agency was created on the Lightspeed computer system. Color ink-jet printouts are output and combined. A pastiche of everyday objects—a hammer, tape rule, apple, architectural blueprints, and a fish—float enigmatically within a computerized photomontage. The coarse reproduction quality, "found" within the printouts, is intriguing within the context of annual report design. Other pages feature digitized European currency, pictures of the New York Stock Exchange, and business equipment. The cover is an unusual combination of heavy pixelation and elegant typography. The alliance continues in the report interior.

Brilliantly colored illustrations have been deliberately created with a large pixel dot. "We could have used a much smaller dot. But we wanted it to be seen. We wanted a coarseness to it" (S. D. Warren Company 1988, 22). Preparation of the final design combined computer and hand processes. After manipulation on the Lightspeed, 3 foot

5-15.

Michael Weymouth Design. Illustration from Annual Report. Massachusetts Industrial Finance Agency. The experimental use of the Lightspeed computer system provided a pixelated coarseness. The 3 foot by 5 foot foot montage was created by hand from color ink-jet printouts. 1987.

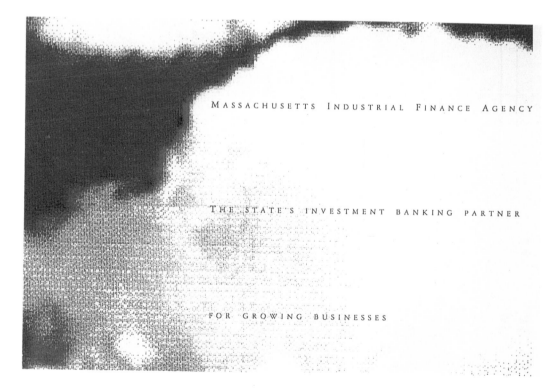

MASSACHUSETTS INDUSTRIAL FINANCE AGENCY

THE STATE'S INVESTMENT BANKING PARTNER

FOR GROWING BUSINESSES

5-16.

Michael Weymouth Design. Cover, Annual Report, Massachusetts Industrial Finance Agency. The large pixel dot was deliberately chosen by the design firm. Coarse texture contrasts with traditional typography. 1987.

5-17.

Michael Weymouth
Design. Interior spread,
Annual Report,
Massachusetts Industrial
Finance Agency. The link
is made between Wall
Street and Main Street.
The pieces of the puzzle
do not quite arrange
themselves into order.
1987.

5-18.

Michael Weymouth
Design. Interior spread,
Annual Report,
Massachusetts Industrial
Finance Agency. Access
to the European money
market is intimated
through digitized currency
and icons of telecom-
munication. 1987.

5-19.

Pentagram/New York.
Peter Harrison, designer.
The pastiche approach in
a Warner Communications
annual report, influenced
by the energy of video and
the memory of torn
theater posters. The torn
paper technique, related
to what Steven Heller has
called the "ransom note
style" of typography, had
been used by Paul Rand in
the 1950s. The idiom
resurfaced and became
increasingly popular
throughout the 1980s. 1987.

by 5 foot prints were ordered and then assembled by hand into large montages. Final art was photographed as 8 inch by 10 inch chromes.

The expressive approach was fostered by both cultural and technological change. Joining Peter Harrison of Pentagram, Rick Valicenti of Thirst, Ernie Perich of Group 243, and Joel Katz of Katz Wheeler Design, Weymouth took the forefront in a chaotic style that reflected and refracted a postindustrial video culture. At its best, concept drove the style. The visual opulence soon deteriorated into the aestheticism of widespread practice. The response of the 1990s, "bare bones" minimalism, was predictable and equally contrived. And, unlike this original work, not particularly risky.

Experimentations with the computer and photographic effects led Weymouth to his solution for a 1988 recruitment brochure. Prepared for the now-defunct Drexel Burnham Lambert, the design rests on the legend, "Everything is in constant motion." A crisp photograph is purposely blurred by waving

hues of color. Typography placed in crooked surprints further obscures the image. Additional questions are raised by a four-sided bleed printed askew. Things are not quite right. In a report for Organogenesis, a firm specializing in organ tissue research, tattered masses surround and frame photographs. Humans have interrupted technological custom. Emulsion that is purposively degraded provides an organic factor consistent with the client's image.

Human demands take precedence. Though exposed, the revelation is distorted. Ironically, the computer is accepted so that Weymouth might best argue against its effects. The cultural erosion of a biotic element is noticed. One cause of that erosion is used against itself. Though his answer is much different than that of Kenneth Hiebert or Clement Mok, Weymouth is engaged in the same confrontation. Technology is believed to be impersonal. Because graphic designers also believe they must find a means to self-expression, this encounter will continue in any possible future.

"The purpose of design is to make our artificial environment more human" (Frolick 1987, 41). Hartmut Esslinger, the founder of frogdesign, understands the essential contradiction in designing for technology. Though we may not fully understand the cause, the intrusion against personal expressiveness and toward visual illiteracy is real. Paralleling the histories of radio and television, a new media is launched as a solution to human communication problems. In each case, from hope has sprung new and vaster wastelands.

Esslinger is well prepared to assume the task at hand. Educated as an electrical engineer and industrial designer at the University of Stuttgart and Fachhochschule fur Design in Gmund, he has reacted against the German design tradition of the Bauhaus, the Ulm School, and Dieter Rams. Establishing his first office in Altensteig, Germany, he founded frogdesign in 1969. The name of the firm is an acronym for Federal Republic of Germany and an allusion to the mascot of the city of Altensteig. Two additional offices, in Carmel, California and in Tokyo, were established in 1982 and 1986. Closely identified with the computer industry, the firm has designed products for Apple, NEC, Epson, Worlds of Wonder, Sony, Sun, Pixar, and NeXT.

The frogdesign response to the computer is to reject the functionalism of Ulm and Rams. Emotion and sensuousness are difficult to project in a pair of rollerskates. Esslinger and his team of "designfrogs" manage to provide a soft-edged, colorful solution which exemplifies the firm's approach. "The biggest cultural task for the designer is to provide a variety of emotions, or feelings, or events. You need symbolism and emotional expression to make a product human" (Aldersey-Williams 1988, 90). Breaking from a tradition of German austerity and graphic purity, frogdesign substitutes rounded edges, ergonomic treatments of the work environment, and the appearance of being small with grace.

The computer, in the form of computer aided design/computer aided manufacturing (CAD/CAM) workstations, permits the creation of humanistic bathtubs, television sets, exercise cycles, cameras, and drinking glasses. Machine tools immediately translate computer sketches into styrofoam models. Designer Herb Pfeifer explains the frog approach to client development: "We don't show sketches. People appreciate models . . . we always have the feeling that the most emotional design gets the highest acceptance" (Aldersey-Williams 1988, 90). After acceptance, the models are reworked on the computer before final plastic prototypes are milled for approval.

Esslinger and frogdesign have been particularly adept in using graphic design and self-promotion to spread awareness of the firm. Instructive use of advertising has stimulated and informed both clients and competitors. The most visible element of the effort has been a continuing series of advertisements run on the back covers of *Form* (West Germany), *ID,* and *Axis.* The symbol of the

5-20.

frogdesign. "Frollerskates," product design
for Indusco, Auburn Heights, Michigan. Soft
edges and colorful plastic are a studio
trademark.

5-22.

frogdesign. Symbol. The omnipresence of the little green frog was self-fulfilling. Esslinger accepted "frogdesign" after Esslinger Design became, by custom rather than definition, the frog design firm.

5-23.

frogdesign. "Rock Hopper." Transportation design study: trial bike "Free Climber." 1990. Photography by Dietmar Henneka. The studio fosters an experimental approach to product development. Ideation is encouraged irrespective of client association. The colorful bike, contrasting with a designer black background, is typical of the frog aesthetic. The design format and visible outline of an 8 inch by 10 inch chrome are repeated month after month, year after year.

5-21.

frogdesign. "14:59." Wondervision, designed for Worlds of Vision. 1987. Levels of reality are connected by red wires falling into the darkness. A pop icon, the Campbell's soup can, is hidden among the shadows at lower right. The can is replicated in Pop Art style on screen.

5-24.

frogdesign. "Frog Net." Industrial design
for The H. Hamlyn Foundation.
Photography by Dietmar Henneka. 1986.
A departure from the humorous approach.
Clarity of meaning is sacrificed to an
unusual postmodernist experiment in
intimation. The revolutionary microchip
claims another victim/victory: a
communications device, part of the
network, emerges from a box more than a
bit too large.

5-25.

frogdesign. "frox in sox in
box." 1987. More typical, a
sample of frog humor. The
tagline at top reads "The
Californian team: 43824
hours in Campbell." That's
5843 days, 1164 weeks.
Esslinger is at top left
(with hand outstretched).
The twenty designfrogs of
the California office
defeat the stereotypes.
Fastened top shirt buttons
and solid black clothing
do not seem to exist at
frogdesign.

firm, a small green frog, was created by scanning a photograph and manipulating the image on computer. Esslinger Design became "frogdesign" serendipitously; when the advertising campaign introduced the ubiquitous frog, the symbol became so popular that the name of the firm was changed.

After several false starts, the sense of the series was established with recent commissions, design studies, upside-down frogs flying over Hawaii, and "frox in sox in box." An entire chrome is printed, including the outer edges of the film, to give the same impression received when viewed on a lightbox. Photography, often the work of Dietmar Henneka, is of exceptional quality. Images are accompanied by a humorous or enigmatic caption, a tagline, and that little green frog.

In an industrial designscape biased toward impersonally engineered severity, several means maintain individuality. Humor, the rounded line in space, and the playfully serious protest are hallmarks. Though recently appropriated by others (especially those who design for the computer industry), the style remains essentially frog. Though daring, frogdesign is not threatening; in fact, its working principles are fundamentally historic. The notion that designers must not allow clients to jeopardize vision is borrowed from Raymond Loewy. The philosophy is an eclectic response to a fluctuating techno-environment. Esslinger believes that, even after success ("a loan from God . . . only possible when you find someone to help you"), "frogdesign is still a protest. . . . We want to prove that we can win without losing our souls" (Frolick 1987, 41).

Within the computer subculture, frogdesign is prototypical. The success of its efforts, and its influence on others, has created a dangerous displacement. Creative concepts become cliches. Unique motifs become commonplace: the unintimidating white chosen for Apple computers, the black for NeXT, a rounded plastic edge, the squared lines cut and pressed into molded surfaces.

The frogdesign "soul," fortunately, is not a limited set of design decisions. Esslinger and his compatriots react against impersonality wherever they find it. Through two decisions, the contradiction between the computer and ourselves is resolved. First, frogdesign creates, for the human being, a sensuous computer. Second, creation assumes both the use of the computer and the personal, emotional commitment of an intelligent, individual designer. The new syllogism: if computer designers are sufficiently human, they are able to humanize the computer.

This is not a guide to choosing a design school. There are, however, few programs globally recognized as having a unique approach to graphic design. The Illinois Institute of Technology (IIT) and its constituent, the Institute of Design, must be included on any short list. In the present context, the Institute's exemplary use of the computer has yielded important results and, perhaps more significantly, paradigms for both graphic design and graphic design education. A view of student work, then, is a preview of design futures.

This should not be surprising. A broad emphasis on computer design is entirely consistent with a heritage of innovation. The reputation and experimental approach of IIT were established by Laszlo Moholy-Nagy and extended by Jay Doblin. The campus was literally built and designed by Mies van der Rohe. Building on the past, the Institute of Design recently inaugurated the first American doctoral program in design.

In a 1985 study, Mihai Nadin and Leif Allmendinger proposed a computer implementation plan for the Rhode Island School of Design (RISD). "Computer technology promises to change the nature of design and participate in the establishment of new forms of graphic expression" (Nadin and Allmendinger 1985, 279). "Non-finite, non-sequential information" created through the computer might "lead us to redefine the main values in the civilization of which it is a component" (Nadin and Allmendinger

1985, 281). Although some insist that the computer is simply a tool, the RISD vision has been accepted and emulated by many. After taking a position at the Institute of Design, Allmendinger joined a faculty including Patrick Whitney, Charles Owen, and John Grimes in following the promise of technology.

A multidimensional, interactive, and nonsequential medium logically engenders myriad applications. Many have already been initiated. As a research facility, various developmental aspects of the computer are being explored at the Institute of Design. Several have not yet begun to reach the mainstream.

Much of this research is interactive and therefore impossible to adequately represent in print. An interactive systems engineer at Apple, Steven Gano, has expressed the differences between traditional graphic design and hyperdesign: "We are near the beginning of an intellectual revolution as sweeping as the one that accompanied the advent of the printed book. For the first time, we will be able to create and arrange events in space and time, and design direct experiences for ourselves and others" (Kunkel 1989, 42). That experience cannot be replicated in this format, the printed book. The design of an image, a consistent part of an interactive physics text, may be appreciated. The interactive design itself cannot be understood.

In unfamiliar territory, the roles of different approaches are often unappreciated.

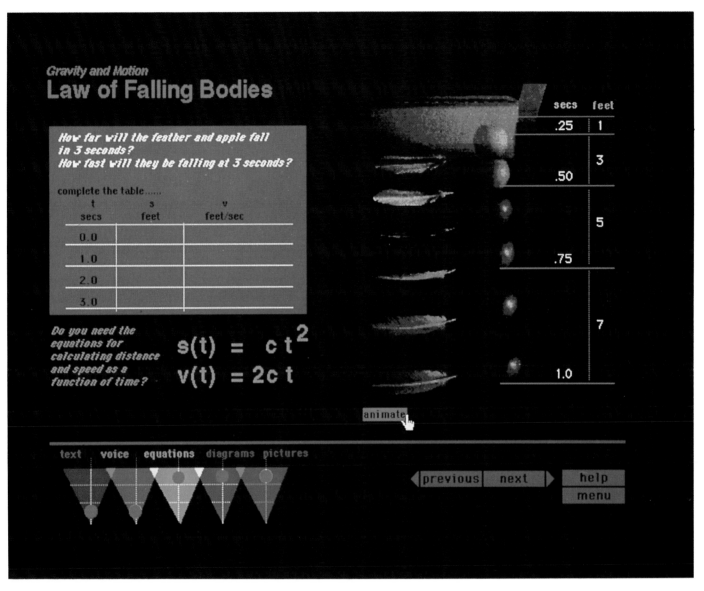

5-26.

Illinois Institute of Technology/Institute of Design. Image from an interactive textbook in physics at the high school level. Pages do not exist in the traditional sense.

Many may now believe that nonsequential interactivity is equivalent to hypermedia. Disparate applications are in fact available; more are being developed. Student designer Miwa Wang has worked through several problems in interactivity. The junior level exercise is a means to teach students how to design computer/human interfaces. Typography and programming are taught concurrently.

A second interactive experiment is a test of an alternative means to navigate through hypermedia. A prototype, designed by student Pamela Mead, requires several levels of decision making. As the viewer moves through information screens, text and data are provided. Possible routes through the software are offered in an open architectural format. At any time, the new reader can seek help, request tools, ask for more information or a review of previous screens, return to the introduction, or search for specific subjects.

Allmendinger has argued that young graphic designers must be prepared for a future in which printing will be made obsolete by computer media. "We have no way of knowing how long printing will last . . . printing's fate is written on the electronic display; as time passes printing's role as the primary communications means will become less and less important . . . it will occupy a role similar to calligraphy and letterpress-printing" (Allmendinger 1991, 14). It may be difficult to believe that printers will become the blacksmiths of the twenty-first century. As we examine hypermedia and other interactive

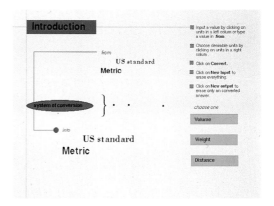

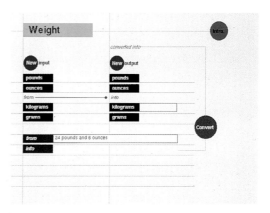

5-27.

Illinois Institute of Technology/Institute of Design. "Introduction." This application teaches students to design appropriate interactions with the computer. Computer/human interface skills must be developed and taught: the transition to a new order requires the mastery of nontraditional abilities. The application converts metric and U.S. standard measurements. Tasks include typographic decision making, programming, and interactivity. Student designer: Miwa Wang.

5-28.

Illinois Institute of Technology/Institute of Design. "Weight." Teaching the design of the human/computer interface. A secondary stage of the interactive programming. Student designer: Miwa Wang.

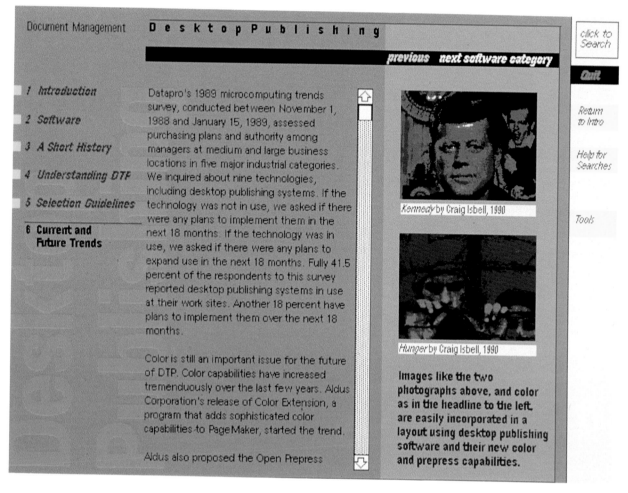

Document Management

D e s k t o p P u b l i s h i n g

previous next software category

click to
Search

Quit

Return
to Intro

Help for
Searches

Tools

1 *Introduction*

2 *Software*

3 *A Short History*

4 *Understanding DTP*

5 *Selection Guidelines*

**6 Current and
Future Trends**

Datapro's 1989 microcomputing trends survey, conducted between November 1, 1988 and January 15, 1989, assessed purchasing plans and authority among managers at medium and large business locations in five major industrial categories. We inquired about nine technologies, including desktop publishing systems. If the technology was not in use, we asked if there were any plans to implement them in the next 18 months. If the technology was in use, we asked if there were any plans to expand use in the next 18 months. Fully 41.5 percent of the respondents to this survey reported desktop publishing systems in use at their work sites. Another 18 percent have plans to implement them over the next 18 months.

Color is still an important issue for the future of DTP. Color capabilities have increased tremenduously over the last few years. Aldus Corporation's release of Color Extension, a program that adds sophisticated color capabilities to PageMaker, started the trend.

Aldus also proposed the Open Prepress

Kennedy by Craig Isbell, 1990

Hunger by Craig Isbell, 1990

Images like the two photographs above, and color as in the headline to the left, are easily incorporated in a layout using desktop publishing software and their new color and prepress capabilities.

5-29.

Illinois Institute of Technology/Institute of Design. A prototype designed to test a navigational approach through hypermedia. The application provides information regarding various software and hardware options. Research was funded by Datapro, a division of McGraw-Hill. Student designer: Pamela Mead.

applications in print, however, we are already experiencing a visual-cultural lag.

VT is a digital imaging system designed and developed by faculty and students of the Institute of Design. Under the direction of Professor John Grimes, students explore the contemporary value of photography. Visual communication traditions are, at times, over-turned. The abandonment of letterpress and foundry type was rapid and permanent. In these works, a transitional phase in the history of photography is investigated. Grimes provides a statement of intent:

> Within the content of computing, the capabili-ties of existing media are so magnified that they cross the boundaries that once separated them from other media. In the extreme case—highly desirable-traditional modes disappear altogether, and the true nature of visual com-munication finally emerges. My work and that of my students pertains to the extension of photography, and more broadly all mechani-cally assisted imaging, into writing, drawing, scripting, and diagramming" (Grimes 1991)

Grimes and his students have devel-oped software pushing the limits of our understanding of photography. Joining an unbroken line of participants as diverse as Henry Peach Robinson, Eadweard Muybridge, Christopher Schad, Man Ray, Duane Michals, and Moholy-Nagy, this work is a continuation and a temporary end.

Institute of Design students are taught, and understand, that graphic design is advo-

5-30.
Illinois Institute of Technology/Institute of Design. VT imagery under the direction of Professor John Grimes. Student designer: Jeffrey Rich.

5-31.
Illinois Institute of Technology/Institute of Design. VT imagery under the direction of Professor John Grimes. Student designer: James Haney.

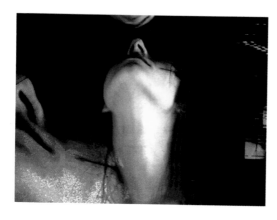

5-32.

Illinois Institute of Technology/Institute of Design. VT imagery under the direction of Professor John Grimes. Student designer: David O'Connell.

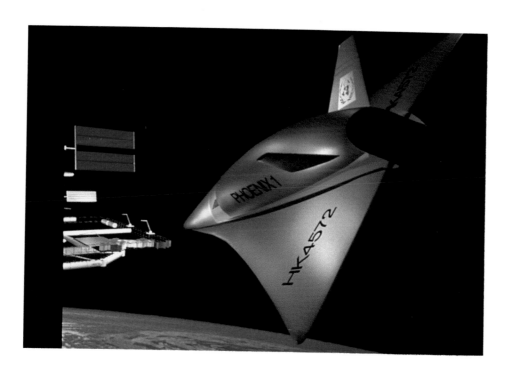

5-33.

Illinois Institute of Technology/Institute of Design. Project Phoenix. "Hypersonic Space Shuttle." Personnel and supplies are brought to orbiting space station. Created with the Silicon Graphics workstation and Alias 2.4. Student team leader: Howard Kavinsky.

cacy. Understanding their responsibility to humanize media, these computer graphic designers have provided remarkable responses. Project Phoenix is an outstanding example of student involvement in socially responsible action. A proposal for an environmentally safe system that permanently generates power, Project Phoenix gives notice of the changing definition of "graphic designer."

That change has in large part been sponsored by the Instititute of Design. The new designer is visionary, planner, facilitator, researcher, and visual communicator. Through Project Phoenix, the problem of global warming is obviated by the elimination of energy production methods requiring carbon dioxide by-products. The project includes space stations, solar power satellites, moon bases, and microwave collection facilities.

Produced with Silicon Graphics microcomputers and Alias 2.4 software, these images exist in an imaginary universe. That potential lives because students have made it to be so. In the past, we were able to create graphics. Today, we can create worlds. There is no better way to comprehend the power of the computer.

Faculty and students at the Institute of Design are participating in a rare opportunity. There are few places as openly interested, or involved, in the process of creation. In the most visionary of places, the lines between future and present must blur. Research becomes reality. Ideas become products. Design has proven that it can provide possible futures. For the most contemporary designers, communication is predictive. Design becomes an allusion to a present we may all soon realize.

AFTERWORD

Computer graphic designers are concerned with an impersonal present and a potential future. For those involved in such serious questions, the question of medium can be insignificant. There is no need to declare oneself a computer user when you are genuinely concerned about global prospects. These futurists and social activists are, nevertheless, computer graphic designers.

We are instructed by our beliefs regarding time. For most of our history, time was not kept by humankind, but by the seasons, the sun, and the moon. Native American cosmologies speak of centuries, of eons of slow change. The season is a basic unit; day and night are mere moments. We continue to accept the inheritance. Anomalous, vacant metaphors inhabit our language. We speak of "sunrise" and "sunset" though, as good Copernicans all, we realize the sun does not move about the earth.

With the industrial revolution came a new order: mechanical time. The 10-hour day, or the 7-hour day, are unnatural, artificial constructs. The time clock signals the debasement of nature.

In a blink—less than two hundred years—mechanical time has been replaced. We speak now of computer time. Digital watches are the new metaphor. We refuse to accept the natural symbology of the circle;

the sweep second hand has become an anachronism. We abandon the need for the natural. Time is now linear, shown in vertical and horizontal rows of liquid crystal display.

In this new time, change is measured more particularly than before. Imperceptibly small moments are counted. They therefore "count"; they assume substance. As our new seasons become progressively smaller, the future is a shorter distance away. Being closer, it is more possible, and more feared.

The computer makes it more difficult to notice the passage from now to then. No longer do we construct images to visualize the speed with which technology moves. There can be no symbol for the nanosecond. We cannot symbolize what we cannot understand. Self-defensively, these computer graphic designers predict the future and thereby create the present. That service is an essential way to make sense.

The medium permits these messages. For designers who confront the zeitgeist of change, the timeliness of the computer is the only reasonable means of communication. Identifying contradictions just before they disappear, we all seek strategies. These designers have found them. Their messages are most significant. We retain just enough of our wits to recognize them, and realize that we must remain human.

6

TYPOGRAPHIC FUTURES

An indication of the distance we have come in two decades: a type designer began one part of his career mastering the art of hand punchcutting. The apprentice learned to physically cut letters into steel. Matrices were made from the punches; metal type was cast in the foundry. The process was fundamentally the same as that of Gutenberg in the mid-fifteenth century.

This type designer, however, is not an Elzevier, or a Caslon, or Didot. In 1965, these fonts were cut by Matthew Carter at the Joh. Enschende en Zonen Foundry in the Netherlands. In 1981, Carter cofounded Bitstream, a company devoted to the production of digital type fonts for laser printers. The movement from individual hot metal letters to digital typefoundries did not occur in generations. It has happened in one career.

Typography and type design are, for the first time in history, being practiced by amateurs. In the early nineteenth century, indenture agreements binding an apprentice to the master piously spoke of the assistant's participation in the "mysteries of printing." By the end of the century, the puzzling etaoin shrdlu keyboards of the Mergenthaler Linotype ensured that typesetting would remain a craft. Learning the discipline of type was a necessary condition for one to even touch the machine. Mastering the use of such expensive mechanical puzzles required years of effort. Craftsmanship was implicit. Though the ancient customs of Joseph Moxon (1683) were not enforced, there remained, among twentieth century compositors, a known canon of custom and appropriateness.

The computer changed all that. Rene Kerfonte, director of typography at Monotype, has recognized the "democraticization of type design." Democracy is a disorderly process. As the technology created means for any user to arrange type on the page, and to alter fonts for personal pleasure, costs are paid. The traditionalist worries that the rules of craftsmanship are being mislaid. The typographically militant argue that such rules were artificial constructs. Many graphic designers take a middle ground, believing an empowered public must be educated. Others guiltlessly participate in the savagery of letterforms.

The "sushi of the nineties," type design offers intriguing choices for both the unsophisticated and the refined. Since the 1970s, typefaces have been produced quickly and cheaply. It is no longer necessary to painstakingly ink original letter patterns, or spend years sketching an alphabet before committing oneself to the metal punch. Phototypesetting technology, lasersetting, and

6-1.
A case study in visual illiteracy. Typography without blame: those who know no better are shown how to batter letters. Detail from poster advertising TypeStyler, a software package that permits manipulation of letterforms. The program is manufactured by Broderbund Software. Three taglines read: "STtyLE aS A CONCEPT. The Stylization Makes The Art. Le Style c'est everything." Primitive computer designers argue that "quality is relative" and that this poster may be reflective of a uniquely contemporary aesthetic. Many disagree. 1990.

software have combined to revolutionize type design. Just as desktop publishing and Aldus PageMaker have changed the way we view the page, Ikarus, Metafont, Novus, Fontographer, FontStudio, FontWare, and TypeStyler have permanently changed the graphic designer's relationship to typefaces.

There are honest differences of opinion regarding the legitimate use of the computer to create and recreate typefaces. Type designers themselves are separated into the two camps of invisibility and visibility. The traditionalists argue that the function of typography is legibility; those who favor a more iconoclastic typography contend that computerized type is a new form not to be judged by ancestral rule. The first metal typefaces were based on calligraphy. Similarly, the first computer typefaces were based on the paradigms of metal. We are now ready, say the extremists, to begin to move away from an outmoded heritage and begin different explorations.

The argument is not a new one. In the 1890s, the complaints of William Morris, Daniel Berkeley Updike, and the private press movement were against the excessively visible forms of Victorian type designers. In the 1920s, Eric Gill and Beatrice Warde espoused a typography that would be completely invisible, a crystal goblet carrying the message without intrusion. The Bauhaus type designers, Paul Renner and Herbert Bayer, disagreed. Forming the persuasive argument that the typeface must reflect contemporary standards, new directions were charted by those who popularized the use of the sans serif. Today's discussion can be framed in similar terms, between those who argue for timeless forms and those who prefer contemporary letters that suit the prevailing mood. For the last two hundred years, the history of graphic design has featured that debate repeatedly.

Contemporary type designers clearly divide themselves. Both camps use the computer to create new letterforms. The tool is restricted by those who continue to participate in a tradition of expressiveness built on grace and elegance. Others make a simpler, more forceful argument. For the newer type designers, the inherent power to communicate must not be leashed. All forms that can be created by the computer should be made available.

As the beneficiaries of two different eras of type design, we live in a fortunate age. The state of this art has been permanently transformed. Unlike any time before the Industrial Revolution, and more dramatically than ever before, we now have categories from which to make choices.

Many argue that choice begets responsibility. The proof is based on classic assumptions of legibility and form. The argument is made that the purpose of the typographic word is, and forever will be, verbal communication. Established standards have served a utilitarian purpose for hundreds of years. To carelessly overturn the precepts of our communicative heritage would be a reckless endangerment of trust. Moreover, visible expressiveness is more appropriately the arena of the fine artist. The responsible type designer prepares those forms able to best carry the rudimentary burden of recognition. The task of the type designer is to construct a new alphabet that serves the purpose of a reading public.

Each designer must decide how persuasive the utilitarian argument becomes. There is, however, an art to the page and the letter. In the traditional forms of type designers who create contemporary letters with the computer, we find timelessness.

Few are able to muster sufficient visual power to convincingly claim that graphic design can be made art. Hermann Zapf is an exception. His elegant vision as typographer, type designer, and calligrapher is consistently dependent on traditional form. He has nevertheless succeeded in his inspection of the contemporary. As a type designer, he has created several of the most popular typefaces of the last several decades. Optima, Palatino, Zapf Book, and Zapf Chancery are as well known to amateur graphic designers as the series of dingbats he designed for International Typeface Corporation in 1977. Both relevant and representative, Zapf succeeds in creating a personal vision of this time.

The designer of over one hundred and fifty typefaces and variations, Zapf has established a contemporary bridge between hand lettering and the laser. A pioneer in the recent renaissance of calligraphy as a vital form of expression, he was also among the first to use the computer to create new typefaces (for many years, beginning in 1977, he taught a seminar in the use of typographic computer programs at the Rochester Institute of Technology). In 1979, Zapf was invited to participate in a cooperative venture with Donald Knuth, the developer of MetaFont and a professor of computer science at Stanford University. The research resulted in a new typeface, Euler, designed with an early prototype of the software system; the face was first used by the American Mathematical Society in 1983. In 1982, Stanford established an important program in digital typography under the direction of Charles Bigelow.

Understanding that technology is a tool, Zapf has acknowledged "the importance of typographic computer programs in the future . . . we have fresh design ideas just as our fellow craftsman did, like Garamond in the Renaissance or William Morris in the nineteenth century" (Zapf 1987, 97–98). He was an early master of both MetaFont and Ikarus, a type design program developed by Peter Karow. His concern for the tradition of craftsmanship, however, has fostered eloquent arguments against unwarranted damage and in favor of a meticulous and ethical approach to the letter. "Manipulation of a type design is a question of ethics, of respect for the designer . . . an alphabet should not be used like chewing gum, bending and stretching it in every direction" (Zapf 1987). Graphic designers, both professional and amateur, now have the ability to alter a typeface at will. The problem has become more evident as new and more powerful software is released. As Zapf observes, "The problems are now very serious. Everybody can alter letterforms, cutting a tail here . . . there is a danger in this development that leads into a wild bastardization of alphabet design" (Zapf 1990, personal letter).

Recognizing that technological piracy is not limited to software, Zapf has been in the forefront of those urging typeface protection through international copyright. He has also recommended that typefaces developed for

THE PRINTER carried on into type the tradition of the calligrapher and of the calligrapher at his best. As this tradition died out in the distance, the craft of the printer declined.

ABCDEFGHIJKLMNOPQRST
¢abcdefghijklmnopqrstuvwxyz
UVWæ + 1234567890 * œ & XYZ

It is the function of the calligrapher to revive and restore the craft of the printer to its original purity of intention and accomplishment. THOMAS J. COBDEN-SANDERSON

6-2.

Hermann Zapf. Page from *Manuale Typographicum* (Frankfurt am Main: Heinrich Egenolf, 1954). The original *Manuale*, commissioned by D. Stempel AG and set in sixteen languages, is a modern classic of the book arts. Quotation is from Thomas J. Cobden-Sanderson, *Ecce Mundus: Industrial Ideals and The Book Beautiful*, London: 1902. The typeface is Cobden-Sanderson's Diotima.

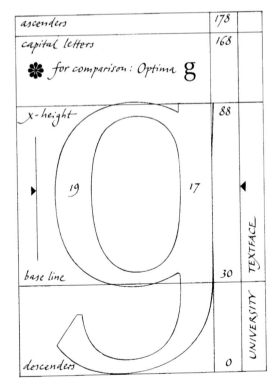

OPTIMA

Optima the newest type design by Hermann Zapf, is a simple yet elegant sans-serif face with subtle shading and balance in its thick and thin strokes. Zapf has achieved a blending of the positive characteristics of Roman and Grotesque with restraint and dignity, attaining a classic immunity to time and fashion.

Optima has been designed in the 20th century idiom. It blends well with the major typefaces in use today, stands up under severe technical tests, and fulfills today's requirements for functional, versatile application.

Optima preserving the color of its Roman origin, combines the simple severe form of classic Roman characters with the dramatic impact of the Grotesque. The result is a practical sans-serif face, just between Roman and Grotesque, which maintains excellent readability without monotony of line.

Optima's extreme simplicity suits it to the printing of technical publications, catalogues or albums, while its charming elegance and restraint provide an equal adaptability to advertising, book or magazine printing. In semi-bold, its rhythmic structure creates an almost Grotesque air.

Optima has been produced in three series: Regular, Italic, Semi Bold; hand type up to 48 point. Italic and Semi Bold in 6 to 12 point contain the same measurements as Regular for easy, time-saving exchange between series. For Linotype composition, matrices are available in 6, 7, 8, 9 and 10 point body size. Inquiries should be directed to the Mergenthaler Linotype Company, 29 Ryerson Street, Brooklyn 5, N.Y.

6-3.
Hermann Zapf. Specimen page for Optima. Mergenthaler Linotype Company. 1960. This face, one of the most popular of modern types, required seven years of effort to perfect. Primary research for the letter was completed between 1952 and 1955; the alphabet was first released in Germany in 1958. Optima was originally designed as a letter to be cast in metal. The type was made available by D. Stempel AG Typefoundry in three weights (regular, italic, and semibold). Additional weights and characters were later added.

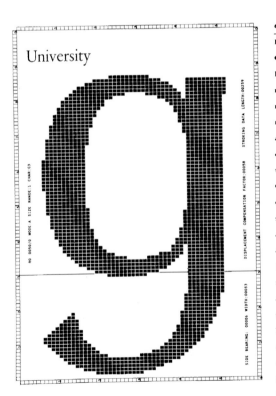

6-4.
Hermann Zapf. University. Optima, a hand-drawn letter, cannot be reproduced at 300-dpi resolution. "The design must be reduced to a heart-breaking compromise. The answer to this problem is that Optima was never designed for digital storage. If I had been asked, I would have done a new design" (Zapf 1987, 104). Pictured is a modified version of a roman face, a simplification of Optima. Zapf is convincing in his argument. His quarrel, of course, is not necessarily against the innovations of Zuzana Licko, Barry Deck, or Max Kisman, but against the "bad and childish" destruction of the crafted letter.

metal typography be adapted to lasersetting, rather than simply copied. The newer, different process requires the creation of designs specifically built for the bitmap: "We should create designs that fit within the structured pattern of the digital principle" (Zapf 1987, 104). Older typefaces must be abandoned or reconstructed to fit new production processes.

Zapf's concern is not universally applauded. The alternative is a universally subjective (and permissive) type design. Fearing the argument for anarchy, most designers demur from the confrontation, complacently accepting the given. Zapf refuses to do so. He has cogently used alphabets created for video display as a case study in support of his claim that quality must be demanded. Acknowledging that compromises must be made, he points out that we seem to accept that the letters we view on screen cannot be better than they are. Such an acquiescence is dangerous: as we lose aesthetic awareness, we accept other losses as well. Refusing to accept "visual pollution," Zapf argues that technology can be properly used to create those alphabets we now require.

MATTHEW CARTER

Personally representing the transition from hot metal to digital typography, Matthew Carter may have been the last person to professionally learn the art of punch cutting. "At the end of a year, I had acquired a skill for which there was no conceivable commercial use" (Gralia 1989, 117). After beginning his vita with an apprenticeship in cutting steel, he has recently (and perhaps paradoxically) taught at Yale University. His teaching technique typifies his approach to letters: he uses Fontographer to provide students with an appreciation of type design. Recognizing traditional standards of typographic beauty and invisibility, he believes that the computer and high-resolution monitor are the ideal tools to design a typeface. "At Yale, students can make acceptable letterforms within a day or two. So, within my experience, the time to conceptualize and produce a real letter has gone from a year to a day" (Coyne 1989, 86).

After moving to New York in 1965, his career as a type designer with Mergenthaler Linotype resulted in several phototypesetting classics. Snell Roundhand, based on a calligraphic script of the late seventeenth century, was designed in 1966 to exploit the ability of a phototypesetting font to join heavily kerned scripts. Bell Centennial was commissioned by AT&T as a new typeface for telephone directories. The digital design was completed in 1978.

With Michael Parker, Cherie Cone, and Rob Freidman, Carter co-founded Bitstream in 1981. The company assists in the desktop publishing revolution by providing digitized versions of typefaces to manufacturers of laser printers. New typefaces have also been designed; the most successful is Bitstream Charter. Over one thousand fonts are now available. In 1988, Bitstream released FontWare, a product that enables personal computer users to make and use their own fonts. While acknowledging that "any fool can make a type design that didn't exist before" (Coyne 1989, 92), Carter believes that such software encourages vitality and energy.

Released in 1987, Bitstream Charter is a case study in the use of new technology to create a commercial typeface. Design decisions were influenced by both aesthetics and the consideration of digital storage. Though more detailed than sans serifs like Helvetica, Charter requires less digital data to describe each character. The ball terminal was sacrificed, replaced by a sheared, angular line. Serifs were designed without curves, as were other parts of letters, including the spurs, beard, ball, nick, and tails. The pragmatically useful result is that the face performs well on both 300-dpi laser printers and high-resolution typesetters. At low-resolution output, straight-line serifs are imprinted without the jagged edges distinctive to curved letterforms.

The original drawings for Charter were made by hand and then digitized. After viewing enlarged letters on the monitor of a computer workstation, characters were output on a plotter. The process of refinement is achieved exclusively through the computer.

acegs

acegs

356

356

hod

hod

hhh**H**

Name   Address   Subcaption   Bold listing

456

6-5.

Matthew Carter. Bell Centennial. The digitization of letters began only after the design concept, submitted through sketches, was approved. Directories are set in six-point type. Letters were first constructed bit by bit, by hand, using graph paper. Given the breadth of Carter's career, it seems appropriate that the process toward digitization should begin with hand-drawn sketches.

❖abcdefghijklmnopqrstuvwxyzåąæ

çđęèfiflfffffifflíijłl·lñœøßųüþð1234567

890ABCDEFGHIJKLMNOPQRSTUVWXY

Z&ÅĄÆÐĘIJŁĿLĽØŒ.,:;-'""!?ABCDEFGHI

JKLMNOPQRSTUVWXYZ&ÅĄÆÐĘ

IJŁĿLĽŒØÞ1234567890£$¥Pt¢ƒ%

‰@#©®©®™.,:;-'""„!?¡¿‹›«»()[]{}

*†‡§¶—abcdefghijklmnopqrstuvwxy

zåąæçđęèfiflfffffifflíijłl·lñœøßųüþð1234

567890 ABCDEFGHIJKLMNOPQRST

UVWXYZ&ÅĄÆÐĘIJŁĿLĽŒØÞ12345

67890£$¥¢ƒ%‰.,:;-'""!?¡¿‹›«»()❖

6-6.
Matthew Carter. Bitstream
Charter. Roman and italic
in complete character
sets. The face was
released in 1987.

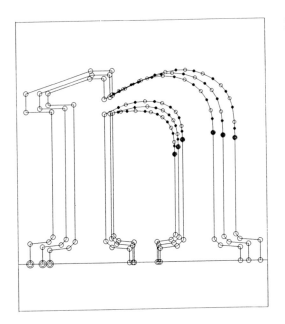

6-7.
Matthew Carter. Bitstream
Charter: the lowercase *n*.
1987. The strength and
simplicity of the design is
offered as a means to
solve the problem of low
resolution. Control points
underscore individual
decisions of the type
designer. Carter used the
Macintosh and a Versatec
plotter in designing the
face. After output was
examined, changes could
be quickly made by
manipulating the shapes
of letters on screen.

Visual variations of bold and italic may be commanded in increments of one percent.

Agreeing with Zapf, Carter believes that new typefaces must be "technology-sensitive without being technology-subservient" (Carter 1990, 61). At reading size, Charter is a solid but simple serif. Created to resolve the specific problems of the digital process, the face is difficult to misuse. That is a significant contribution. Carter has tackled the task of educating new designers. The range of quality exhibited in Bitstream typefaces is an important advance toward that goal. As a type designer and principal in a digital type-foundry, Carter has begun to provide a formula by which beginners can prevent their own mistakes.

The biography of a computer type designer does not require that they begin their career as a calligrapher. Judging from the short list of Zapf, Carter, and Stone, however, it does seem probable. Sumner Stone discovered an interest in typographic form while a student at Reed College in Oregon. His studies with calligrapher Lloyd Reynolds prompted a short career as a lettering artist with Hallmark Cards. His interest in typography led him to found the Alpha and Omega Press in Sonoma, California in 1972. By 1981, after completing graduate study in mathematics, Stone became interested in computer typography. In 1984 he was named director of typography of Adobe Systems, the manufacturer of the PostScript page description language.

Selling typefaces to a public less sophisticated than the professional graphic designer, Adobe's corporate design program has at times been suspect. The digital foundry has, however, supported traditional type values. That contribution has, if not empowered, been at least mirrored in the beliefs of Sumner Stone.

Adobe and Stone reclaimed the truth of the past by conducting research into the history of such classic faces as Garamond. In 1541 Claude Garamond designed the first typeface not based specifically on handwriting—the first true printing face. Dominant until the mid-eighteenth century, modern versions of Garamond are based on the 1615 recutting of Jean Jannon and an American

Type Founders revival of 1898. Rather than copying from copies, Adobe based their version of the face directly on type cast from the original punches and matrices in the Plantin-Moretus Museum in Antwerp. The Vraye Parangonne (approximately eighteen point) was chosen as representative. Adobe's historic research has repaired the damage done to other faces as well, including types originally cut for Kis, Caslon, and Granjon.

Adobe has also produced two collections of American nineteenth century faces, Wood Type I and Wood Type II. The faces are based on original alphabets supplied by Rob Roy Kelly, contemporary specimen books, and the National Museum of American History. Although many believe that such faces should not have existed in the first place, the decision to translate these alphabets required an admirable appreciation for the expressiveness of the typographic original.

In 1988, Adobe produced an original of its own. Five graphic designers were asked to participate in the creation of the Adobe Playing Card Deck. Gail Blumberg and Joss Bratt Parsey designed the suit of diamonds; Russell Brown, the hearts; Ruth Kedar, the spades; and Paul Woods, the clubs. Using Adobe Illustrator 88, PostScript, Display PostScript, and Adobe Separator, the new computer graphic designers produced cards that were alternatively witty, exploratory, retro, and typographic. The deck rapidly became a design collectible. More significantly, the project was successful in fostering a discussion of soft-

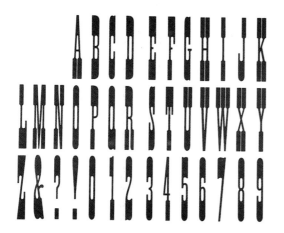

6-8.

Adobe Systems. Ponderosa, released as part of Adobe's Wood Type I collection. 1990. This software package includes five typefaces, Juniper, Cottonwood, Ponderosa, Mesquite, and Ironwood, along with ornaments complementing the type styles. The faces were designed by Kim Buker, Barbara Lind, and Joy Redick under the direction of Fred Brady and Carol Twombly. The bases for these letters were American nineteenth century vernacular faces; specimens were provided by Rob Roy Kelly.

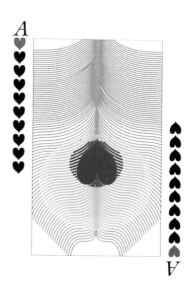

6-9.

Russell Brown, designer. Adobe Systems. Selection from the Adobe Playing Card Deck: the queen, king, and ace of hearts. From the Adobe deck: "My goal was to show off the range and subtlety of colors possible using Adobe Illustrator 88, as well as to have some fun with the transformation tool" (Adobe Systems, 1988).

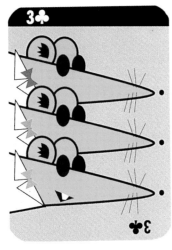

6-10.

Paul Woods, Woods &
Woods, designer. Adobe
Systems. Selection from
the Adobe Playing Card
Deck: the three, four, and
five of clubs. "I illustrated
the ideas, things or
thoughts associated with
the number" (Adobe 1988).
Woods added two left
feet, a five-star general, a
six-pack, the seven days of
the week, a billiard eight
ball, a cat with nine lives,
and ten little Indians to
the images shown.

6-11.

Ruth Kedar, designer.
Adobe Systems. Selection
from the Adobe Playing
Card Deck: the queen and
king of spades. "I am
amazed at the amount of
precision and fine detail I
can achieve with this
software; it takes the
drudgery out of much of
the painstaking work
involved in making
illustrations" (Adobe
1988).

ware potential among graphic designers. Though not as interesting in terms of inherent design quality, a poster series (playing on such themes as "Doing It With Type" and "Bending Rules") and the Adobe Type Catalog, a periodical produced by Adobe's in-house design studio, has performed a similar service. In one poster, however, Sumner Stone is captured by Lance Hidy in a fittingly expressive design statement.

Stone extended the definition of a typeface in 1988. He began designing an alphabet in 1984, shortly after his arrival at Adobe. Understanding that a family of type includes the several different variations in weight and attitude (regular, bold and black; roman and italic; condensed and extended), each family has consisted of a set of patterns based on a single design. That design was restricted. The letters in a serif family were all serifs; sans serifs were, by definition and by custom, faces of a different order.

Stone offered a new proposal. His Stone family consists of a serif, a sans serif, and an informal which are structurally and procedurally consolidated. Certain characteristics, including x-height, cap height, and stem weight, are identical. Though the three branches of the family have different purposes, they may work together. "I designed the Stone Family to integrate these three different letterform styles . . . many kinds of typography produced today can benefit from the use of such a comprehensive family" (Stone 1991, 12).

The design of the typeface involved a working process often used by those who

6-12.
Adobe Systems. Cover of the Fall 1990 issue of *Font & Function*, the Adobe type catalog.

6-13.
Sumner Stone, examining a letter on screen. The Macintosh and Adobe Illustrator 88 are used to refine the drawn characters

STONE SERIF

ABCDEFGHIJKLMNOPQRSTUVWXYZ
abcdefghijklmnopqrstuvwxyz
fiflß æœ ÆŒ àèíöûñç ÀÈÍÖÜÑÇ
1234567890& .,:;'""'- – —?!/)]}◊«»
$¢£¥ƒ†‡*§¶%@#

ABCDEFGHIJKLMNOPQRSTUVWXYZ
abcdefghijklmnopqrstuvwxyz
fiflß æœ ÆŒ àèíöûñç ÀÈÍÖÜÑÇ
1234567890& .,:;'""'- – —?!/)]}◊«»
$¢£¥ƒ†‡*§¶%@#

ABCDEFGHIJKLMNOPQRSTUVWXYZ
abcdefghijklmnopqrstuvwxyz
fiflß æœ ÆŒ àèíöûñç ÀÈÍÖÜÑÇ
1234567890& .,:;'""'- – —?!/)]}◊«»
$¢£¥ƒ†‡*§¶%@#

STONE SANS

ABCDEFGHIJKLMNOPQRSTUVWXYZ
abcdefghijklmnopqrstuvwxyz
fiflß æœ ÆŒ àèíöûñç ÀÈÍÖÜÑÇ
1234567890& .,:;'""'- – —?!/)]}◊«»
$¢£¥ƒ†‡*§¶%@#

ABCDEFGHIJKLMNOPQRSTUVWXYZ
abcdefghijklmnopqrstuvwxyz
fiflß æœ ÆŒ àèíöûñç ÀÈÍÖÜÑÇ
1234567890& .,:;'""'- – —?!/)]}◊«»
$¢£¥ƒ†‡*§¶%@#

ABCDEFGHIJKLMNOPQRSTUVWXYZ
abcdefghijklmnopqrstuvwxyz
fiflß æœ ÆŒ àèíöûñç ÀÈÍÖÜÑÇ
1234567890& .,:;'""'- – —?!/)]}◊«»
$¢£¥ƒ†‡*§¶%@#

STONE INFORMAL

ABCDEFGHIJKLMNOPQRSTUVWXYZ
abcdefghijklmnopqrstuvwxyz
fiflß æœ ÆŒ àèíöûñç ÀÈÍÖÜÑÇ
1234567890& .,:;'""'- – —?!/)]}◊«»
$¢£¥ƒ†‡*§¶%@#

ABCDEFGHIJKLMNOPQRSTUVWXYZ
abcdefghijklmnopqrstuvwxyz
fiflß æœ ÆŒ àèíöûñç ÀÈÍÖÜÑÇ
1234567890& .,:;'""'- – —?!/)]}◊«»
$¢£¥ƒ†‡*§¶%@#

ABCDEFGHIJKLMNOPQRSTUVWXYZ
abcdefghijklmnopqrstuvwxyz
fiflß æœ ÆŒ àèíöûñç ÀÈÍÖÜÑÇ
1234567890& .,:;'""'- – —?!/)]}◊«»
$¢£¥ƒ†‡*§¶%@#

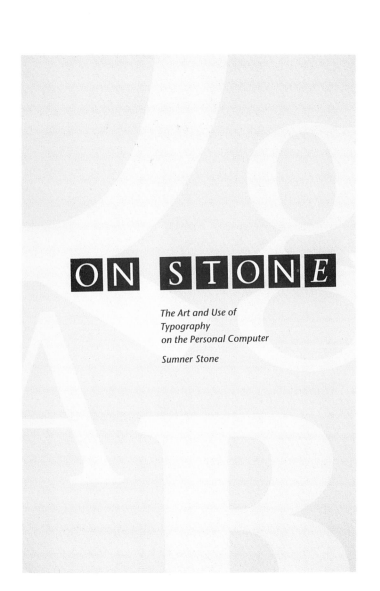

ON STONE

*The Art and Use of
Typography
on the Personal Computer*

Sumner Stone

6-14.

Sumner Stone. Stone Serif shown in medium, semibold, and bold. The family consists of three variants, each available in three weights, and in roman and italic. Illustrations adapted from *On Stone*, published in 1991 by Bedford Arts, Publishers, San Francisco. 1988 (above left).

6-15.

Sumner Stone. Stone Sans shown in medium, semibold, and bold. 1988. (above center).

6-16.

Sumner Stone. Stone Informal shown in medium, semibold, and bold. 1988 (above right).

6-17.

Sumner Stone. The cover of *On Stone: The Art and Use of Typography on the Personal Computer.* Designed by Stone and Kenneth Wu, this is an exceptional introduction to a traditional design aesthetic. Sections include "Thoughts on Stone," "Working with Stone," and "Looking at Stone." The second section features examples of the Stone family in use. Information design, books, periodicals, signage systems, corporate identity, invitations, and artistic works have been prepared and reproduced as examples of appropriate usage. 1991.

have embraced computer graphic design. The first step was sketching by hand.

> I started drawing with a pencil and paper. First I drew about a hundred characters, each with a lowercase height of about one inch. I had these characters photographically enlarged to six times their original size, and then made precise redrawings by hand. These large pencil drawings were then digitized by plotting many points along the outline of a character with a digitizing tablet. The coordinates of these points were stored in the computer. From the original one hundred pencil-drawn characters, now manipulable in computer form, the entire typeface grew. (Stone 1991, 16)

After digitization, the letter can be viewed "larger-than-life" on the computer screen; minute manipulations are possible. Signaling the changing nature of graphic design and typography, the Stone family is more malleable than its progenitors. Our preconceptions concerning what a typeface is, or should be, have changed.

Though a different stratagem, these typefaces share the responsibility assumed by Bitstream Charter. They cannot be easily corrupted. Stone's interest in educating the newly designing public has continued. After leaving Adobe Systems in January 1990, he established Stone Type Foundry in Palo Alto, California. He also completed a project begun in 1987. *On Stone: The Art and Use of Typography on the Personal Computer* is a primer of graphic design. Set primarily in Stone, the book is "intended to serve typographers and graphic designers as a window onto the typographic stage" (Stone 1991, 20). The beautifully printed and designed product of lasersetting is entirely consistent with the author's attitudes regarding the creative process. Designed by Stone and Yale graduate Kenneth Wu, the book reflects "the attention to detail of the professional typographer" and the "loving care of the master" (Stone 1991, 8). We are fortunate to have three exemplars, in Stone's work, the *Hybrid Imagery* of April Greiman, and the *Graphic Design Processes* of Kenneth Hiebert, of both the book arts and the "creative impetus that springs from our mind and soul" (Stone 1991, 9).

Educated at the Rietveld Academy in Amsterdam in the 1960s, Gerhard Unger understood the meaning of contrast. The polarity between traditional and contemporary was conspicuous. He attempted to glean the best from both sides of the spectrum. After working at Total Design, one of the studios leading the way for the Dutch typographic avant garde, he taught at the Academy and learned at the Enschende type foundry. By 1975, he had established a long association with Rudolf Hell GmbH, a German manufacturer of digital typesetters. Unfortunately, his typefaces were little known beyond those few who could afford to purchase these expensive machines of unrivaled distinction. Unger's designs for Hell included Demos, Praxis, Hollander, Flora, Swift, and Cyrano.

Unger has mastered the art of the digitized type design. He is currently working on two faces, Amerigo and Oranda, designed specifically for low-resolution printers. He has recently completed work on Argo, a digital typeface for Hell and URW of Hamburg. His earlier work, however, is his initial claim as a computer type designer. Designed in the 1970s, Demos is a product of both heritage and high tech. Recognizing the coarse rasters of cathode-ray tube technology, he created a strong letter that could withstand fast printing on poor paper. However, as Unger points out, the face proudly stands in a tradition of "clarity, sturdiness, straightforwardness

. . . all this is characteristic of Dutch type design over some four hundred years" (Kinross 1991, 38). Anticipating the extension of family developed in Stone and Lucida, Demos is part of a collection of typefaces, including Praxis and Flora, that were designed to harmoniously co-exist on the page.

Fortunately, we have now begun to appreciate this work. New opportunities have been created by desktop publishing and the adoption of PostScript as an industry-wide standard. Unger's typefaces, designed decades ago, are now for the first time available to a wide audience. Recognizing that his types were created with an allegiance to a technology antecedent but related to laser-writing, several digital type foundries have now released them. Unger continues to work on future projects. We can therefore expect that the work of both his past and future will continue to receive warranted recognition.

The demand for quality in typeface design has increased. Flirting with the ebullient New York expressiveness of Herb Lubalin, Ed Benguiat and the recent Retro stylists, with thousands of evermore outrageous display faces, has become more circumspect. The work of thoughtful designers and calligraphers receives greater attention. Adrian Frutiger, Carol Twombly, Robert Slimbach, Neville Brody, and Garret Boge have contributed in discriminate ways toward a continuation of the trend.

Demos

abcdefghijklmnopqrstuvwxyz
ABCDEFGHIJKLMNOPQRSTUVWXYZ

abcdefghijklmnopqrstuvwxyz
ABCDEFGHIJKLMNOPQRSTUVWXYZ

abcdefghijklmnopqrstuvwxyz
ABCDEFGHIJKLMNOPQRSTUVWXYZ

Praxis

abcdefghijklmnopqrstuvwxyz
ABCDEFGHIJKLMNOPQRSTUVWXYZ

abcdefghijklmnopqrstuvwxyz
ABCDEFGHIJKLMNOPQRSTUVWXYZ

abcdefghijklmnopqrstuvwxyz
ABCDEFGHIJKLMNOPQRSTUVWXYZ

6-18.
Gerhard Unger. Demos, a
traditional Dutch serif,
and Praxis, its sans serif
companion. The faces
were originally designed
for Rudolf Hell GmbH in
the 1970s and have
recently been made
widely available through
the standards of
PostScript and desktop
publishing.

The guild mentality is still strong among the typographic community. Craftsmanship continues as a treasured virtue. There is an exhibited reverence for typefaces, a feeling that does not easily allow the essentially experimental attitude of those who believe letters must be expressively visible. Many among us would not dare to design a typeface.

These traditionalists may be faced with the prospect of becoming a dwindling majority. Whether through ignorance or courage, those who newly come to graphic design, through the computer, are not as hesitant to investigate holy places. They are joined by professionals who express serious doubts regarding the sacredness of any typeface. This growing minority is buttressed by new forms and new type designers. Often, the lines between the two camps are hazily drawn. Each use the same technology; each speaks of the same advantages, offering letters to be best used and manufactured by the computer and within the computer age.

The way we think about typefaces has been changed. For the first time in history, any graphic designer—today, anyone—is able to create a typeface. No union card is necessary to operate the new machine.

Much of this change has happened because of the work of a very few type designers. Unquestionably, Zuzana Licko is the leader among those who would change our attitudes concerning type design. Born in Czechoslovakia, Licko cofounded Emigre Graphics with Rudy VanderLans in 1984. As typographer and type designer for *Emigre,* she has provided original, computer-generated typefaces that comprise a significant component of the magazine's visual language.

Recognizing the limitations of the computer, Licko rejects the conventional response. Rather than attempting to repair or prevent the damage, she exploits the liability, creating faces designed to work best when output on low-resolution printers. Traditional faces are not repudiated because of aesthetics. It is aesthetics itself that is rejected. "Quality is not an absolute" (Berry 1991, 24).

Believing with VanderLans that the familiar is the most legible, Licko argues that standards of clarity and legibility are subjective. Habit creates standards: "This is what makes certain typestyles more legible or comfortable: You read best what you read most" (Emigre Graphics 1990, 13). Typefaces should not be judged according to precepts determined by an obsolete technology or outmoded fashion. "Typefaces which we perceive as illegible today may well become tomorrow's classic choices. Blackletter typestyles which we find illegible were actually preferred over more humanistic designs during the fourteenth and fifteenth centuries" (Cleary 1990, 50).

Just as VanderLans provides patterns to be copied by his public, Licko has become responsible for the work of many type designers sharing her views. Her first faces

No.14/$7.95

6-19.
Zuzana Licko. Heritage. The illustrative
letters were created by bitmapping a
blackletter typeface. Used as the cover
typography of *Emigre 14: Heritage*. The
issue is a survey of young Swiss graphic
designers. Wolfgang Weingart, Hamish
Stuart, April Greiman, Hans-Rudolf Lutz,
and others are interviewed by the
principals of Emigre Graphics. 1990.

were prototypically built on the bitmap. Emperor 8 and Emperor 15, numbered according to their pixel-height, were the first two typefaces. "Coarse resolution has been a great source of inspiration for Emigre Fonts. We began our type design exploration with several low resolution bitmap faces as alternatives to the standard dot matrix faces. Later, we derived many of our high resolution designs from the proportions of bitmaps" (Emigre Graphics 1991). Using Apple's Font Editor, Licko creates algorithms to fabricate a basic structure. The decision-making process is often quite similar to those of the traditionalists. She has added serifs, for example, to sharpen low-resolution corners, the same reason serifs were originally used by Roman stonecutters.

Emigre fonts are internationally available through FontShop, digital type foundries, and directly from Emigre Graphics (catalogs are available in both traditional paper and as an animated HyperCard stack). The paper catalog offers an informative survey of purpose and methods. Licko provides comments, explanations, and definitions. "Digital technology has advanced the state of graphic art by a quantum leap into the future. Ironically, this has turned designers back to the most primitive of graphic ideas . . . designers must reconsider basic rules previously taken for granted" (Emigre Graphics, 1991). Discussing Citizen, she notes that "the smooth printing option provided by Macintosh was the inspiration" (Emigre Graphics, 1991). Citizen was designed to take advantage of the newfound ability to translit-

6-20.

Zuzana Licko. Universal/Citizen. A two-page spread from the Emigre Graphics catalog. Universal is based on Licko's first typeface, Emperor. The two variations of Universal are 8 and 19, referring to the number of pixel units required to create cap height. Universal Eight was the foundation of Citizen, created by using the Macintosh "smoothing" routine. Pixels are polished into "smooth diagonal and circular segments." 1991.

6-21.

Zuzana Licko. Citizen. A visual description of the polishing process. "The shapes of Citizen were generated by smoothing a coarse bitmap, enlarging it approximately four times, and then smoothing it again (shown). The double "smooth" contours appeared as straight lines of varying length and angles, which were then converted into outline form." (*Emigre 15: do you read me?*) 1990.

CITIZEN

DESIGNED BY ZUZANA LICKO
AVAILABLE AUGUST 1990

ggg (FIGURE 1)

THE DESIGN OF CITIZEN (FIGURE 2) IS A DIRECT RESULT OF THE "SMOOTH" PRINTING OPTION PROVIDED BY THE APPLE LASERWRITER. THIS FEATURE OFFERS A SHORTCUT TO INCREASING THE RESOLUTION OF BITMAP TYPEFACES FROM SCREEN TO PRINTER. THE 72 DPI BITMAPS ARE PROCESSED INTO 300 DPI BITMAPS, THEREBY CREATING THE ILLUSION OF HIGH RESOLUTION PRINTING. THE SHAPES OF CITIZEN WERE GENERATED BY SMOOTHING A COARSE BITMAP, ENLARGING IT APPROXIMATELY FOUR TIMES, AND THEN SMOOTHING IT AGAIN (FIGURE 1). THE DOUBLE "SMOOTH" CONTOURS APPEARED AS STRAIGHT LINES OF VARYING LENGTH AND ANGLES, WHICH WERE THEN CONVERTED INTO OUTLINE FORM.

Ay Citizen bold or...

AaBbCcDdEeFfGgHhIiJjKkLlMmNnOoPpQqRrSsTtUuVvWwXxYyZz
1234567890

(FIGURE 2)

...Light

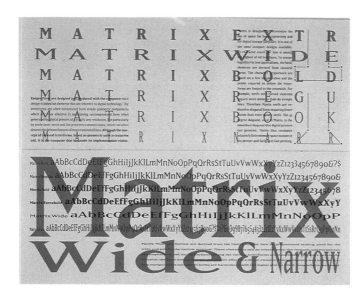

6-23.
Zuzana Licko. Oblong/
Elektrix/Lunatix. Two-
page spread from the
Emigre Graphics catalog. It
is perhaps too traditional
to refer to these faces as
created for display
purposes. From the
catalog: "On the electronic
page, text and image are
once again created
simultaneously with the
same medium, bringing
back greater control."
"The adaptation of our
alphabet to today's
digital technology is re-
evaluating the traditions
in which today's
letterforms are still deeply
rooted." 1991.

6-22.
Zuzana Licko. Matrix. A
two-page spread from the
Emigre Graphics catalog.
The family is shown in
single-line display at top:
narrow, book, regular,
bold, wide, and extrabold.
This is Licko's most
traditional face. She uses a
strategy similar to that of
Matthew Carter in the
design of Bitstream
Charter. From the Emigre
catalog: "To economize the
use of space for both
typesetting and for digital
storage purposes . . . Matrix
serifs are reduced to
diagonal lines, requiring
fewer points than even
square serifs." 1991.

erate 72 dpi to 300 dpi, creating the illusion of medium resolution. The shapes were created by smoothing the letters of a low-resolution typeface, Emperor, into a series of angled straight lines.

Recently Licko has designed different letters for a range of resolution options: low, medium, and high. High-resolution faces, such as Modula, Matrix, and Triplex, have been popular among traditional type users. Modula is available in either a sans or a sans serif version. Matrix (the face you are now reading) has been produced as a family; variations include Book, Bold, Wide, Narrow, and Tall. The face is available in both Apple and IBM formats. Italics need not be designed; software allows the user to slant letters on command. Display typefaces have also been created, including Elektrix and Oblong. Though these faces betray no obvious beginnings in the bitmap, their angular edges are attempts to "maximize the use of digital technology" (Emigre Graphics, 1991).

For Licko, the need to create typefaces was not based on any aesthetic desires. She decided to solve a problem others said could not be resolved.

> When nobody else is able to make something work, I get inspired to find out what I might do with it. I heard everybody say how bad digital type looked and how it was impossible to make it look any better. This really intrigued me . . . I saw there was something unexplored and interesting there and I wanted to try my hand at it. That's when I got involved with designing my first low resolution type. (Emigre 1990, 10)

After understanding the problem, she created a unique solution. In any society, in any culture, the unique will be understood, by some, as appalling.

Displayed as specimens, Licko faces seem to mesh within the tradition. In use, the typefaces are more shocking. The VanderLans designs discussed in Chapter 2 are usually expressed through these faces. Licko understands, and appears to enjoy, the iconoclastic nature of these investigations. A standard motif of the private press, the combination of red and black, is abused in the catalog. The word "heritage" becomes the genesis for an experiment in wild illegibility.

VanderLans and Licko are succeeding in their attempt to disturb a drowsy typographic world. This is not change for the sake of change. Emigre Graphics is using technology to create a new expressiveness. Along the way, they have led others toward new possibility.

As thousands of designers ordered Emigre fonts, an aesthetic was being created. That style has been fostered by the publication in *Emigre* of experimental typefaces, by work published in computer magazines, and by the interest of a growing coterie of computer type designers more interested in personal expression than in legibility. Although much of this work is difficult to discover, several designers have established themselves as potential contributors to a primitive future. Max Kisman, discussed in Chapter 2, has participated in the discussion. A member of the Ambassadors of Aesthetics, a Dutch design collective which published the irregular journal *TYP/Typografisch papier,* Kisman has maintained that some typefaces should be designed for one purpose and then be discarded. Several of his typefaces are scheduled for distribution by the FontShop.

"I need a steady diet of fonts that are weird enough for me to really enjoy using," writes Barry Deck (*Emigre 15*). The creation of fresh ideas can be demanding. While completing coursework at CalArts, Deck developed a proficiency with Fontographer. He has since completed several typefaces, including Barry Sans Serif, Canicopulis Script, Industry Sans Serif, and Template Gothic. The last is based on naive lettering he had noticed on a discarded laundry sign. The type "reflects Deck's interest in type that is not perfect; type that reflects more truly the imperfect language of an imperfect world inhabited by imperfect beings" (Emigre Graphics 1991).

The computer has permitted the freedom to determine a personal visual direction. Deck's offering of the typeface to the public does not imply an interest in serving the aesthetic needs of others. Consistently subjective, he believes the graphic designer must satisfy himself: "I just try to design alphabets that I'd like to use. I am doing it for me. I am not doing it for traditional type designers" (*Emigre 15*). Template Gothic has recently been added to the Emigre font library.

Jeff Keedy agrees with the notion that individual experience must be inserted within the typeface. "People think of the computer as being an impersonal, cold and calculating machine, but ironically, it allows for a great deal of irregularity and personal expression" (*Emigre 15*). NeoTheo is based on the letterforms of the Dutch founder of de Stijl, Theo van Doesburg. The reflection of tradition is a continuing strain among those who reject it. Deck's Canicopulis Script, for example, is based on Gill Sans. Licko's Totally Gothic was built on the foundation of a blackletter script.

Having designed several successful faces, Keedy has struggled to avoid convention while maintaining a connection to audience. A typeface that began as Bondage, and became Keedy, has been scheduled for release by Cipher (Keedy's own type foundry) and the Emigre Library. Although many of his typeface designs are jarring, Keedy has also produced Manuscript, a remarkably tame sans serif. He contends that type designers

●Template Gothic

Template Gothic AaBbCcDdEeFFgGHhIiIjJkKhLmMnNnOoOpPqQrRsStTtUuVvWwWxXyYzZ1234567890&

Template Gothic Bold AaBbCcDdeEfFgGhHiIjKkLlMmNoOpPqQrRsStTuVvWwWxXyYzZ123l45678

Barry Deck's homage to the vernacular. "There was a sign in the
laundromat where I do my laundry," Deck explains, "The sign was done with lettering
templates and it was exquisite. It had obviously been done by someone who was totally
naive. A few months ago, it was replaced with a plastic sign painted by a skilled sign painter.
I asked them if I could have the old sign, and they gladly handed it over to me. Now its on
the wall in my bedroom." Deck was thus inspired to design a face that looked as if it had
suffered the distortive ravages of photomechanical reproduction. The resulting Template
Gothic typeface reflects Deck's interest in type that is not perfect; type that reflects more
truly the imperfect language of an imperfect world inhabited by imperfect beings.

6-24.
Barry Deck. Template
Gothic. Homage to the
vernacular, from the
Emigre Graphics catalog:
"There was a sign in the
laundromat where I do
my laundry. The sign was
done with lettering
templates and it was
exquisite. It had obviously
been done by someone
who was totally naive."
1991.

introduced his typeface, everyone was saying: "Oh god, what an ugly typeface!" Actually, it's possible that
in thirty or forty years people might think of my typefaces as elegant. You have to look at them in the context of time. Eventually they might even be stodgy, old typefaces. Emigre: *Baskerville* eventually became a
good typeface because it was used a lot. I don't think it is intrinsically a legible typeface. People just became familiar with it by default. When you promote the idea that designers should get more involved in designing their own typefaces and personalizing them, are you not worried that if everyone does their own
type, the audience will never really get used to any of them, and subsequently will have a harder time
reading? Mr. Keedy: **There will never be a font that is as
pervasive as *Helvetica* again, because there
are going to be just too many typefaces out
there, too many designers wanting to do
things that are specific. And what that
means is that communication will get a little
closer to ideas. Ideas are very specific.
Places are specific. Why should every air-
port sign system on the planet be designed
with *Helvetica*?** Emigre: Because, especially with sign systems, people have to be able
to read information in a split second and *Helvetica* has been forced down everybody's throat, and has
therefore become a very recognizable and easy-to-read typeface. Don't you feel that if every designer designs his or her own typefaces, and you have all these voices speaking, that the audience is going to have a
hard time constantly adjusting to all these variations on the same theme? Don't you think you make things
more complex by adding yet another typeface, yet another variation? Mr. Keedy: **Maybe it's
making things more complex, but it is also
making things more specific, and in that
sense I can say it is making things clearer.** It is
the Modernist argument that designers need to promote clarity, serving human advancement. To them, civilization is always moving forward and improving. I don't necessarily agree with that, either. I think there
are a lot of voices that have not been heard typographically. Whenever I start a new job and try to pick a

6-25.
Jeff Keedy. Keedy,
released in 1991. The
typeface, originally known
as Bondage, used here in a
page from *Emigre*. 1991.

have unwisely permitted themselves and their types to be cast in specific roles. In an indefinite and complex life, that is a mistake. Through ambiguity, the type designer can create spaces in which individuals make decisions. Interpretation is a necessary step in the information process. Graphic designers cannot and do not impose communicative order. At its best, design is an affirmative act, permitting ideas to take shape and become personal. These type designers do not believe they are responsible for the interpretative acts of the audience.

There is freedom in the loss of responsibility. Emancipated from obligation, primitive type designers can openly express themselves. There is, of course, some danger in complete autonomy. Joined by many who demand one route toward exploration of the personal, Licko is to be congratulated for her courage and her success.

We have become uncertain of our own roles. Arguing that uncertainty should not be a basis for conservatism, Licko and her supporters believe the good they do is to provide avenues for the individual viewer to participate more fully in the act of communication. The means and the matter of discourse has been changed irrevocably. The recognition of that change becomes the infrastructure of a new type design.

Ironically, this rejection of a perceived artificiality may be defended by history. The letters of the constructed typographic tradition are static, figuratively constituted in metal. The source of these forms, however, is the quill. In the more remote past, calligraphic models were more expressive, more personal than the typefaces that followed. Today, human needs demand the creation of a malleable typeface. Calligraphy suited the same, specifically human requirement. The motivation of the radical type designer is not new. It has merely resurfaced in the anonymity and impersonalism of contemporary culture.

AFTERWORD

There is no arbitrator of type design, no means through which we can determine who makes the better argument. Computerization has established two different establishments, the old and the new. They will, at least for the foreseeable future, co-exist.

The brightest designers understand the pleasure of this circumstance. Each understands the contributions of the other. There are no arguments between Zapf and Licko. Those who make the greatest contribution need not be troubled with grievances against those who have honestly proceeded in a different direction. Originality is not blocked by variation. Armed with a personal vision, each has accomplished what they set out to do.

The philosophical paradox is that the visible and the invisible share the same needs. The traditionalist and the primitive, Zapf and Licko, each wish to express themselves. They express themselves differently. There is little more to be said. It is wonderful that the computer has allowed this to happen.

7 AFTERWORDS

We are not yet after words. Words remain. There are different ways to produce words. Human involvement is the constant.

In my last book, I concluded with thoughts concerning the contemporary state of graphic design. "The printed word changed our relationship with one another and with society, but today, that relationship is threatened by malleable words and messages. Text printed on the computer screen is more illusive, more subjective, than the printed word. This is the beginning of a new exploration" (Labuz 1991, 148). If that is a conclusion, this book is not. Because this is not a report on the contemporary scene, but on the future. The graphic designers discussed in this book, artists all, are universally predictive. They are visionaries with specific ideas about where they, and we, are headed.

As a technologist, I have been confronted for twenty years by the computer. Each successive advance has fostered the prediction of another. Some forecasts have proven correct. But how many times have I heard that voice-activated typesetting will be the next wave? That by 1990, or 1992, or 1994, we all will be speaking to our monitors rather than creating keystrokes by hand? Or that by 1995, libraries lined with pulp will be obsolete, replaced by videotext and unlimited computer memory?

At times, the futurist forgets an essential human characteristic. We are damnably difficult to predict. The future will certainly continue the exploration already begun. The most significant advances of our history may be made by hypermedia. Nonlinear, participatory information processes may revolutionize the way in which graphic design is created, known, and understood. New truths will be revealed in each reading of the interactive text. Will this change the world? Perhaps. Every new medium has changed the world.

There are constants. We will not see, any time soon, the death of print. The emotional attachment to paper seems, at least for me, a natural extension of our demand for tactile sensation. We will continue to appreciate the works of master designers simply because, let's face it, we like to look at them. Function is an intellectual mechanism. As professionals, we understand its importance. The emotional pleasure we

receive from the well-crafted page or the appropriate symbol nevertheless remains.

The different arts exist because they must. They will continue to do so. Each performs its own service, communicating in a specific and exquisitely unique manner. Graphic design, which Roger Remington has defined as the alliance of type, photography, and illustration, will continue. Technology may alter the manner in which designed communication is created and received. It cannot alter the basic human need to communicate. The computer is revolutionary. It is not so powerful that it can change our nature.

Graphic designers have not settled on how we will master the machine. Different visions are brought to bear. How will we use the computer, now and tomorrow, to communicate? That, the central question of this book, may already have been correctly answered. But we can't know who has done so.

We do know that we are not after words. Irrespective of the relativism and subjectivism that batter our age, we develop new means to bring messages. We still try to communicate. For one, I am quite comfortable in believing that we are successful in doing so. The chain remains unbroken.

BIBLIOGRAPHY

Chapter 1

Hugh Aldersey-Williams. *New American Design.* New York: Rizzoli, 1988.

Hugh Aldersey-Williams. Social Science. *ID: International Design,* January/February 1987, 38–43.

Muriel Cooper. Computers and Design. Special issue of *Design Quarterly,* Number 142, 1989.

L. Mills Davis. *Toward The Electronic Studio.* Washington, DC: Davis, 1986.

Meredith Davis. Are We More, or Less, Alike? *Statements: A Publication of the American Center for Design,.* VII:1, Fall 1991, 20–21.

Joseph Deken. *Computer Images: State of the Art.* New York: Stewart, Tabori & Chang, 1983.

Stephen Heller. "Muriel Cooper." In Mildred Friedman (editor), *Graphic Design in America: A Visual Language History.* Minneapolis: Walker Art Center, 1989, 96–99.

Edward Gottschall. *Graphic Communications '80s.* Englewood Cliffs, NJ: Prentice-Hall, 1980.

Douglas Hofstadter. Meta-Font, Metamathematics, and Metaphysics: Comments on Donald Knuth's "The Concepts of A Meta-Font". *Visible Language*, XVI:4, Autumn 1982, 309–338.

Donald Knuth. The Concept of A Meta-Font. *Visible Language*, XVI:1, Winter 1982, 3–27.

Donald Knuth. *The Metafont Book*. Reading, MA: Addison-Wesley, 1986.

Ronald Labuz. *Contemporary Graphic Design*. New York: Van Nostrand Reinhold, 1991.

Ronald Labuz. *How To Typeset from A Word Processor*. New York: R.R. Bowker, 1984.

Gary Ludwig. Comments for the Nineties. *ID: The Magazine of International Design*, VIII:3, May/June 1990, 54.

Wendy Richmond. Computers in the Studio: Burns, Connacher & Waldron. *Communication Arts*, May/June 1989.

Chapter 2

Hugh Aldersey-Williams. London Report: Graphic Design. *ID: Magazine of International Design*, March/April 1989, 48–53.

Giorgio Camuffo. *Pacific Wave: California Graphic Design*. Udine, Italy: Magnus Edizioni, 1987.

Mark Fulton. John Hersey. *Communication Arts*, XXX:8, January/February 1989, 94–101.

Sally Price. *Primitive Art in Civilized Places*. Chicago: University of Chicago Press, 1989.

William Rubin. *Primitivism in Twentieth Century Art*. New York: Museum of Modern Art, 1984. (Two volumes).

Rudy VanderLans. *Emigre*, Volumes 1–18, passim.

Rudy VanderLans and Zuzana Licko. The New Primitives. *ID: Magazine of International Design*, March/April 1988, 58–61.

Chapter 3

Hugh Aldersey-Williams. *New American Design: Products and Graphics for a Post-Industrial Age*. New York: Rizzoli, 1988.

Anonymous. Kazumasa Nagai. *Communication Arts*, January/February 1983, 42–45.

Bill Bonnell and Stephan Geissbuhler. New Wave in Graphic Design. *Graphis*, 229 (February), 38–49.

Chuck Byrne. Miss April. *Print*, April 1987, 120.

Rob Carter. "April Greiman." In *American Typography Today*. New York: Van Nostrand Reinhold, 1989.

Anne de Forest. Myths and Misconceptions: California Graphic Design. *ID: Magazine of International Design*, January/February 1990, 46–51.

Rudolph de Harak. *Posters by Members of the Alliance Graphique Internationale 1960–1985*. New York: Rizzoli, 1986.

John Folis. Takenobu Igarashi. *Graphis*, Number 205, February 1979/1980.

Edward Gottschall. *Typographic Communications Today*. New York: International Typeface Corporation, 1989.

April Greiman. *Does It Make Sense?* Special issue of *Design Quarterly*, No. 133, 1986.

April Greiman. *Hybrid Imagery: The fusion of technology and graphic design.* New York: Watson-Guptill, 1990.

April Greiman. Intuition Guides Analysis. *Design Journal,* Society of Typographic Arts, 1987, 58–67.

Annette Hanna. April Greiman. *ID: Magazine of International Design,* March/April 1987, 54–59.

Steven Heller. "April Greiman: An Interview." In Mildred Friedman (editor), *Graphic Design In America.* Minneapolis: Walker Art Center, 1989.

Takenobu Igarashi. *Igarashi Alphabets.* Zurich: ABC Editions, 1987.

Takenobu Igarashi. *Space Graphics.* Tokyo: Shoten Kenchiku-sha, 1983.

Kazumasa Nagai. *The Works of Kazumasa Nagai.* Tokyo: Kodansha, 1985.

Kazumasa Nagai and Yusuke Kaji. *Publications and Advertising Work from Shiseido.* Tokyo: Kyuryudo Art Publishing, 1986.

Gerry Rosentsweig. "April Greiman." In *Graphic Design Los Angeles.* New York: Madison Square Press, 1988.

Penny Sparke. *Modern Japanese Design.* New York: Dutton, 1987.

Richard S. Thornton. *The Graphic Spirit of Japan.* New York: Van Nostrand Reinhold, 1991.

Shigeru Uchida. Recent Works of Takenobu Igarashi. *Idea,* Number 171, 1983.

Wolfgang Weingart. *How Can One Make Swiss Typography?* Basel: Allgemeine Kunstgewerbeschule, 1972–1976.

Wolfgang Weingart. *Projects: Typographic Research at the School of Design, Basel.* Neiderteufen, Switzerland: Allgemeine Kuntsgewerbeschule, 1979.

Chapter 4

Mikkel Aaland. MacDesign. *Graphis,* 259, January/February 1989, 44–56.

Hugh Aldersey-Williams. "Skolos Wedell and Raynor." In *New American Design.* New York: Rizzoli, 1988.

Valerie Francene Brooks. Information's Architect: Richard Saul Wurman. *Print,* XLIV:V, September/October 1990, 120–129.

Dick Calderhead. The Art of Advertising Apple. *Graphis,* 259, January/February 1989, 57–63.

Hugh Dubberly. "An Introduction to Hypermedia and the Implications of Technology of Graphic Design Education." In *Pedagogy in Graphic Design: Proceedings of the Annual National Symposia 1989.* Minneapolis: Graphic Design Education Association, 1991.

Hugh Dubberly. The Future of Writing and Designing with Computers. *AIGA Journal of Graphic Design,* VI:4, 1989.

Nathan Felde. Lance Hidy. *Communication Arts,* January/February 1984, 44–51.

Alan Fern. *Lance Hidy's Posters.* Natick, MA: Alphabet Press, 1983.

Gail Deibler Finke. The Mirage and Clement Mok. *How: Ideas and Techniques in Graphic Design,* VI:5, July/August 1991, 70–75.

Kenneth Hiebert. *Graphic Design Processes . . . Universal to Unique.* New York: Van Nostrand Reinhold, 1992.

Kenneth Hiebert. Structure and Freedom in Design. Unpublished lecture delivered at "Universal/Unique," The University of the Arts, Philadelphia, February 1988.

Nigel Holmes. *Designer's Guide to Creating Charts & Diagrams.* New York: Watson-Guptill, 1984.

Montieth M. Illingworth. Design Along the Strip (Clement Mok). *How: Ideas and Techniques in Graphic Design,* VI:5, July/August 1991, 70–75.

Katherine McCoy. Digital Graphic Design: Educating A New Design Professional. *Statements: A Publication of the American Center for Design,* VI:2, Winter 1991, 6–9.

Roy McKelvey. "Digital Typography: The Peculiarities of Simulated Materials and Tools." In *Defining the Boundaries: Proceedings of the Annual National Symposia 1990.* Minneapolis: Graphic Design Education Association, 1991.

Clement Mok. "Statement. In Giorgio Camuffo" (editor), *Pacific Wave: California Graphic Design.* Udine, Italy: Magnus Edizione, 1987.

Ken Morris. The Information Designers. *Other Criteria: The American Center for Design Journal,* 1:1990, 30–41.

Robert A. Parker. Skolos, Wedell + Raynor. *Communication Arts,* January/February 1990, 82–91.

Chee Pearlman. Apple By Design. *ID: Magazine of International Design,* September/October 1989, 37–41.

John F. Sherman. "Our Need for Digital Craft." In *Defining the Boundaries: Proceedings of the Annual National Symposia 1990.* Minneapolis: Graphic Design Education Association, 1991.

David C. Traub. Neomedia and Hypermedia: What's in a Word? *Verbum: The Journal of Personal Computer Aesthetics,* 4:1, 1990, 30–31.

Edward Tufte. *Envisioning Information.* Cheshire, CT.: Graphics Press, 1990.

Richard Saul Wurman. *Rome Access.* New York: Access Press, Ltd., 1987. Access Press publications have been produced for New York, Los Angeles, Washington, Paris, Rome, Tokyo and many other cities.

Richard Saul Wurman. *US Road Atlas 1990.* New York: Access Press, Ltd., 1990.

Chapter 5

Hugh Aldersey-Williams. London Report: Graphic Design. *ID: Magazine of International Design,* 36:2, March/April 1989, 48–53.

Hugh Aldersey-Williams. "frogdesign." In *New American Design: Products and Graphics for a Post-Industrial Age.* New York: Rizzoli, 1988, 90–95.

Leif Allmendinger. Computer Supported Media Will Make Printing Obsolete. *Statements: A Publication of the American Center for Design,* VI:2, Winter 1991, 13–15.

Leif Allmendinger. Design Education and New Media. *Statements: A Publication of the American Center for Design,* VII:1, Fall 1991, 16–19.

Stephen Bayley. *The Conran Directory of Design.* New York: Villard Books, 1985.

Hugh Dubberly. Hypertext: The Future of Writing and Designing with Computers. Unpublished paper.

Stephen I. Frolick. frogdesign: The World According to Esslinger. *Graphis,* March/April 1987, 38–51.

Simon Johnston, Mark Holt, Michael Burke, and Hamish Muir. *8vo: An International Journal of Typography.* Passim.

Paul Kunkel. Hyper Media. *ID: Magazine of International Design,* 36:2, March/April 1989, 40–44.

Mihai Nadin and Leif Allmendinger. Computers in Design Education: A Case Study. *Visible Language,* XIX:2, Spring 1985, 272–287.

Chee Pearlman. The Next Contender. *ID: Magazine of International Design,* 36:1, January/February 1989, 46–51.

Sharon Helmer Poggenpohl. Graphic Design: Computer Graphics. What Do They Mean and How Do They Fit. *Visible Language,* XIX:2, Spring 1985, 178–225.

Rudy VanderLans. A Conversation with Hamish Muir: 8vo. *Emigre 11: Heritage* (1990), 20–23.

S.D. Warren Company. *Annual Report Trends 7.* Boston: S.D. Warren, 1988.

Chapter 6

Adobe Systems, Inc. *Font & Function: The Adobe Type Catalog.* Mountain View, CA: Adobe Systems. Periodical.

John Berry. A Renaissance in Type Design. *Aldus,* March/April 1991, 22–26.

Charles Bigelow and Lynn Ruggles, guest editors. *Visible Language,* XIX:1, Winter 1985. A special issue, "The Computer and The Hand in Type Design," partial proceedings of the Fifth ATypI Working Seminar. Included are articles by John Dreyfus, Hermann Zapf, Donald Knuth, Matthew Carter, and Edward Gottschall.

Gail Blumberg and Joss Bratt Barsey, Russell Brown, Ruth Kedar, and Paul Woods, Woods & Woods. *The Adobe Playing Card Deck.* Mountain View, CA: Adobe Systems, 1988.

Chuck Byrne. Adobe's Design. *Print,* XLIII:11, March/April 1989, 76–83.

Matthew Carter. Typography and Current Technologies. *Design Quarterly 148: The Evolution of American Typography.* Minneapolis: Walker Art Center, 1990.

Sebastian Carter. *Twentieth Century Type Designers.* New York: Taplinger Publishing Co., 1987.

Ed Cleary. Typography: Elektrix Shock. *Studio,* VIII:5, September/October 1990, 48–50.

Richard Coyne. Matthew Carter. *Communication Arts,* XXX:8, January/February 1989, 86–93.

Michelle-Anne Daupe. Get The Message? Legibility Is Relative. *eye,* 3:1, Spring 1991, 4–7.

John Dreyfus and Knut Erichson. *ABC-XYZapf: Fifty Years in Alphabet Design.* London: The Wynken de Worde Society, 1989.

Emigre Graphics. Conversation with Zuzana Licko. *Emigre 15: do you read me?* 1990, 6–13.

Emigre Graphics. *The Emigre Catalog.* Berkeley, CA: Emigre Graphics, 1991.

Preston Gralia. Man of Letters: Matthew Carter. *PC Computing,* January 1989, 118–24.

Karrie Jacobs. A Conversation About Type. *Emigre 15: do you read me?* 1990, 18–19.

Karrie Jacobs. An Existentialist Guide to Type. *Metropolis,* April 1988, 45–49, 65–68, 81.

Robin Kinross. Technology, Aesthetics and Type: Gerard Unger. *eye,* 3:1, Spring 1991, 36–43.

Donald Knuth and Hermann Zapf. AMS Euler—A New Typeface for Mathematics. *Scholarly Publishing,* XX:3, April 1989.

Peter Mertens, Legibility. *Emigre 15: do you read me?* 1990, 4–7.

Richard Rubinstein. *Digital Typography: An Introduction to Type and Composition in Computer Systems Design.* Reading, MA: Addison-Wesley, 1988.

Sumner Stone. *On Stone: The Art and Use of Typography on the Personal Computer.* San Francisco: Bedford Arts, 1991.

Sumner Stone. The Type Craftsman in the Computer Era. *Print,* XLIII:II, March/April 1989, 84–91.

Rudy VanderLans and Zuzana Licko. *Emigre 15: do you read me?* 1990.

Rudy VanderLans and Zuzana Licko. *The Emigre Catalog.* Berkeley, CA: Emigre Graphics, 1991.

Hermann Zapf. *Hermann Zapf and His Design Philosophy.* Chicago: Society of Typographic Arts, 1987. Pertinent chapters include "The Designer in the World of Metafont" and "Future Tendencies in Type Design: The Scientific Approach to Letterforms."

Hermann Zapf. Unpublished keynote address at Type '87. New York. October 12, 1987.

Hermann Zapf. *Hora fugit—Carpe diem. Ein Arbeitsbericht.* Hamburg: Maximilian-Gesellschaft, 1984.

COLOPHON

This book was written with an AST Premium 386/SX personal computer, an IBM Portable PC, an AST Premium Exec notebook, and a Zydos 386 notebook. WordPerfect version 5.1 was used for text processing. The manuscript was delivered to the publisher in both paper and diskette form. Both the writing and the design were executed in DOS format.

During the design phase of the project, Don Dempsey and the author used an AST Premium 486 personal computer to visualize possibilities and prepare layouts. The AST notebook was used to transport electronic files for remote printing. The computer system used to complete the design was not purchased specifically for this project; however, during the design process, a new Radius full-page pivot monitor was acquired to allow greater on-screen visibility of the electronic pages. The system runs at 33 Mhz, with a 200MB Connor hard drive and an external Bernoulli Transportable 90MB drive.

Aldus PageMaker (version 4.0), CorelDraw 2.0, PhotoStyler 1.0, and Logitech Ansel were run in Microsoft Windows 3.1 to facilitate the process. The designers created macro formats of verso and recto pages. Two-page layouts were prepared and manipulated on screen. Software permitted illustrations to be placed, cropped, and sized with much greater speed than otherwise possible. Desktop design proved to be an ideal means to resolve the restrictive nature of the verso/recto format chosen by the designers.

Proofs were output in two forms. Preliminary layouts were accessed through an AST Turbolaser/PS plain paper printer; final color proofs were output with the QMS Color-Script 100. The Emigre fonts used in this book were purchased specifically for the project and were loaded as resident fonts in PageMaker through Adobe Type Manager 2.0 and were then downloaded to the printers. Adobe Type Manager and a full-page monitor permitted the designers to accurately visualize all typography.

A Microtek 300Z scanner, loaded with PhotoStyler, was used to scan art. Text was imported directly into Page-Maker as required. All art was scanned at 108 dpi resolution.

In some cases, a Vivitar Instant Slide Printer was used to produce photographic copies of art to be scanned. Although all the art was scanned, art was furnished as original color copies, as chromes and as digital art on diskette.

The resident memory required for the project necessitated the use of the Bernoulli. In order to work efficiently, graphics were stored in the Bernoulli system and then imported into PageMaker as required. Files were backed up to minidata cartridge tapes using a Colorado tape drive and PC Tools Backup for Windows.

All typefaces set for this book were created by Zuzana Licko (the faces are available in both Macintosh and IBM format from Emigre Graphics). With the exception of the vertical titles identifying the graphic designers, the Matrix family has been used. Matrix was chosen in part for aesthetic reasons but also because it was specifically created for the purposes of computer graphic design. Matrix serifs require less storage space than other serifs; there is a resulting economy for both typesetting and digital storage. Body copy is set 12-point Matrix Book with a 17-point linespace. Captions are set in 6-point Matrix Wide with a 12-point linespace and Matrix Wide Bold with a half-point rule. Folios are reversed in 8-point Matrix Wide. Running heads are also set in 8-point Matrix Wide, with a half-point rule. Chapter titles are reversed in red, set in 24-point Matrix Wide Bold. The family was created without italics; as good traditionalists, the designers requested and received permission from Licko to slant the face in order to create pseudo-italics when required. The vertical titles are set in 30-point Emperor Fifteen. The font has no lowercase characters.

Proofing was permitted in part through the use of the computer design facilities of the Department of Advertising Design at Mohawk Valley Community College. In addition to the Turbolaser and the ColorScript printers, a Linotronic 200P was used to create typeset-quality spreads for initial design approval. For review purposes, spreads were produced and output in paginated form.